Walk!

Exmoor

with

David & Carol Hitt

DISCOVERY WALKING GUIDES LTD

Walk! Exmoor
First Edition - April 2006
Copyright © 2006

Published by
Discovery Walking Guides Ltd
10 Tennyson Close, Northampton NN5 7HJ,
England

Photographs*
All photographs in this book were taken by the
authors.
Front Cover Photographs

Walk 29   **Walk 6**

Walk 16   **Walks 8 & 27**

ISBN 1-904946-18-6

Text and photographs* © David & Carol Hitt

Walk!
Exmoor

CONTENTS

David and Carol, both born in Exeter, were brought up with a love of the Devon coast and countryside. Although their work took them abroad and to other parts of England, they always vowed to return to their home county. After busy business careers they welcomed an opportunity to live in Mid Devon and now enjoy a more relaxed pace of life in a small friendly village.

They are keen walkers and relished the challenge of becoming members of the Discovery Walking Guide team to rediscover the beauty of Exmoor. David works as a Security Management Consultant and Carol is involved with local voluntary community projects. Any spare time is taken up by attempting to tame their one-acre wilderness, otherwise known as the garden.

Dedication
For our granddaughter Maysa, the light of our lives, born between researching walks 10 and 11!

Acknowledgements

Patrick for his wit, wisdom, companionship and sharing his love of Exmoor, but thankfully not his rock cakes!
David and Ros for their vision, professional support, patience and good humour.
For long-suffering family and friends who have endured months of endless stories about our research and escapades.
To friendly walkers we met en-route who shared enthusiasm and knowledge.
The National Park Authority for conserving and enhancing Exmoor's natural beauty, wildlife and cultural heritage.

INTRODUCTION

On a clear blue-sky day, we are taping our first impressions of Walk 29 at **County Gate**. Starting high above wooded slopes of the curving **East Lyn Valley** and gazing around a terrific moorland horizon, our recording begins, "wow, what a fabulous view".

... wildness and softness interwoven ...

Beside us, a more eloquent description is engraved on the viewpoint indicator, "I do not know of any other comparable area where such wildness and such softness are so closely interwoven" the author J H B Peel (1913-1983) wrote in his Portrait of Exmoor. And it's this striking contrast and variety of intertwined landscapes which gives Exmoor its remarkable appeal and offers such a richly rewarding and stimulating area for adventurous walkers.

There's wildness on the desolate moorland plateau and along rugged cliff tops, each offering an expansive feel and miles of fine distant views. One of the joys of Exmoor is the seamless, flowing connection between moors and cliffs, whilst at the same time, cutting through them, are winding valleys that provide a more gentle, intimate landscape. We round each bend with a thrill of anticipation, wondering what new secret will be revealed.

We often use the word 'suddenly' in our route descriptions, because part of Exmoor's endearing attraction are the rapid changes in its landscapes. Emerging from the tree line of a wooded *combe*, we are straight onto the moor; rounding a coastal headland, we plunge into a wooded river valley, while on leaving a pasture, we suddenly descend a sunken lane into a hidden *cleave* - such quick transitions make for invigorating and interesting walking.

Rounding a headland, plunging into the Heddon Valley

The glorious coast, looking towards Great Hangman

Given its compact size, Exmoor certainly punches above its weight as a walking destination; for us, the icing on the cake is its glorious coast, though whatever your taste, there'll be something to delight you.

WALKING ON EXMOOR

If variety is the spice of life, then Exmoor, England's smallest National Park provides a wealth of spicy walking; signed paths and trails cross high moors, wind through steep sided *combes* and stretch along a stirring coastline. Until the mid 19th century, Exmoor could only be crossed on horseback or foot along centuries-old ridge trails, military roads and sunken lanes; today, hikers use these ancient byways and are spoilt for choice with over 1000 miles of well maintained tracks, bridleways and paths.

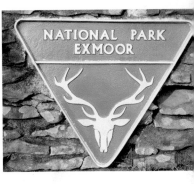

Minehead, the start of the South-West Coast Path

There is excellent year round walking and many routes stay quiet throughout the seasons; even those passing through main tourist attractions are often busy only on summer weekends and Bank Holidays.

Where possible we offer a variety of walking within a route and have included a range of distances plus shorter versions and extensions; the majority of ascents and descents are steady. Some walks follow parts of the six long distance trails that cross Exmoor. Unless otherwise indicated, timings reflect our walking pace without stops, so we suggest you check your timings against ours early on in the route.

Right to Roam has doubled the amount of Access Land available, although landowners had previously allowed access on much of this newly designated land. Please be aware however, that Access Land may occasionally be closed, as may access to permitted paths.

An access land logo

GEOLOGY AND GEOGRAPHY

Exmoor's 267 square miles straddle north Devon and west Somerset; much of the privately owned land is used for sheep and cattle farming. The region is basically a large plateau of sedimentary rocks laid down in the Devonian period some 400 million years ago; erosion has formed several long ridges and valleys behind high northern sea cliffs. An immense tidal flow into the funnel of the **Bristol Channel** causes the second highest tidal range in the world, a neat trick of nature to prevent the over-development of the coastline.

The coast

The 35-mile coastline between **Combe Martin** and **Minehead** is simply magnificent. Broad, open downs topped by the south-west's highest cliffs lie between **Combe Martin** and the aptly named **Woody Bay**, where trees cover the slopes to **Lee Bay**. After the unique **Valley of Rocks** and imposing **Countisbury Hill**, more wooded slopes sweep through **Culbone** to the wide **Vale of Porlock**, before stark cliffs continue to **Minehead Bay**.

The magnificent coastline towards Lee Bay (Walk 19)

On clear days there are extensive views to **Lundy Island** and across the **Bristol Channel** to the **Brecon Beacons** and **Gower** peninsula.

The inland moors and hills

The road from Dunkery Beacon to Porlock Vale

Behind the coast a high plateau stretches south east to **Dulverton**. The moors lying north of a line between **Blackmoor Gate**, **Simonsbath**, **Exford** and **Wheddon Cross** are big remote spaces offering splendid hiking country and Exmoor's highest summit at

Dunkery Beacon. Heading south, a broad ridge running from **Shoulsbury Common** to **East Anstey Common** marks the south-west edge of the National Park. To the east of **Wheddon Cross** lie the softer **Brendon Hills**, with a lush patchwork quilt of fields along the **Luxborough Valley**.

A typical lush patchwork quilt

The rivers

The northern valleys of the **East Lyn**, **Hoaroak Water** and **Heddon** contain wonderful spirited rivers which concentrate their beauty and power into a short headlong dash from **The Chains** to the **Bristol Channel**. **The Chains** are also the source of the southward flowing rivers, particularly the **Exe** and **Barle** (see the photo on the next page) which have longer to develop their characters along twisting moorland valleys, before joining forces just below **Dulverton**.

MAN ON EXMOOR: FARMING AND TOURISM

Man has inhabited, cultivated and mined Exmoor for thousands of years, proof of which exists in the form of burial mounds, field cultivation systems, Iron Age settlements and WW11 fortifications. The most significant recent effects on the landscape occurred in the 19th century when the Knight family purchased the ancient Royal Forest in the centre of the moor. Their introduction of livestock farms with fields surrounded by beech hedges still exist today. Victorian engineering ingenuity also attempted to extract minerals on a greater scale than previously but today there are only remnants of disused structures.

The twisting Barle Valley (Walk 34)

A combination of the Romantic poets, 18th century unrest in Europe and the Napoleonic Wars started the region's tourist industry. Coleridge, Southey, Shelley and Wordsworth all stayed in

The natural beauty of the coast at Trentishoe Down

the area and waxed lyrical about its natural beauty. The romantic notion of Exmoor was reenforced in 1869 when R D Blackmore published his famous novel 'Lorna Doone - a romance of Exmoor' which continues to capture both the essence of the landscape and the reader's imagination.

Today, tourism and leisure is key to the success of the local economy. Popular tourist spots include; **Watersmeet**, the **Valley of Rocks**, **Doone Valley**, **Dulverton**, **Dunster**, **Lynton** & **Lynmouth**, **Selworthy**, **Porlock Vale**, **Horner** and **Dunkery Beacon**.

Whilst many visitors associate Exmoor with Lorna Doone, **Tarr Steps Clapper Bridge**, Exmoor Ponies and Red Deer, the region has far more hidden delights, best explored on foot.

Tom's Hill Barrows (Walks 11 & 37)

Amongst our favourite 'off the beaten track' gems covered in our routes are; **Tom's Hill Barrows** and **Badgworthy Water**, **Farley Water**, **Cheriton Ridge** to **Hoar Oak**, **Upper Barle Valley** to **Cornham Brake**, **County Gate** and the **East Lyn Valley**, the **Rugged Coast Path**, **Holdstone Hill**, the ruined village of **Clicket**, **Winsford** and **Bye Common** and **Heddon's Mouth**.

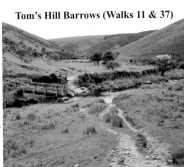

A passion for Cream Teas

Selworthy Green - ideal for cream teas

Exmoor's fragile rural economy is under threat. Please support local enterprises and buy local produce and goods where possible. We freely admit to overindulgence in cream teas; our passion for Exmoor is only equalled by our desire (mainly David's) for discovering the perfect summer afternoon scone and cuppa. The question is, cream or jam first? We recommend plastering the scone with cream prevents it crumbling too quickly before adding a good dollop of jam!

FLORA AND FAUNA

Bossington (Walks 2 & 40)

Herds of hardy Exmoor ponies, Britain's oldest equine race and an endangered species, are dotted across the moor; fond of gorse, their grazing habits aid land conservation. Red deer are harder to spot but there's a chance with a pair of binoculars, particularly during the autumn rutting season when the belling (roaring) of the stag is an unforgettable sound.

Over 200 species of birds have been identified. Seabirds and waders can be seen on **Porlock**'s salt marshes and skylarks still provide a welcome summer song soaring high above the moors. Butterflies and moths abound and include the rare Heath Fritillary butterfly.

A combination of undisturbed landscape and clean air encourages the growth of many rare plant species, lichens and ferns; many Sites of Special Scientific Interest have been created to protect unique and rare environments.

OTHER ACTIVITIES

There are plenty of excellent attractions; fascinating historic sites, pretty villages and lively market towns, arts and craft centres as well as gardens to wander around at leisure. Outdoor activities include cycling, horse riding, shooting, river and sea fishing, coastal boat trips, wild life parks and safaris. Several interesting heritage centres and exhibitions celebrate local history and rural life. Railway enthusiasts, well catered for, should refer to the Appendix G. What's on information is available in Tourist Information Centres and the free 'Exmoor Visitor' magazine.

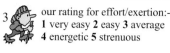 our rating for effort/exertion:-
1 very easy **2** easy **3** average
4 energetic **5** strenuous

 approximate **time** to complete a walk (compare your times against ours early in a walk) - does not include stopping time

 approximate walking **distance** in miles/kilometres

approximate **ascents/descents** in metres (N=negligible)

circular route **linear** route **figure of eight** route risk of **vertigo**

 refreshments (may be at start or end of a route only)

- Walk descriptions include:
- timing in minutes, shown as (40M)
- compass directions, shown as (NW)
- heights in metres, shown as (1355m)
- GPS waypoints, shown as (Wp.3)

Notes on the text
Place names are shown in **bold text**, except where we refer to a written sign, when they are enclosed in single quotation marks. Local or unusual words are shown in *italics*, and are explained in the accompanying text.

All the map sections which accompany the detailed walk descriptions in Walk! Exmoor are reproduced under Ordnance Survey licence from the digital versions of the latest Explorer 1:25,000 scale maps. Each map section is then re-scaled to the 40,000 scale used in DWG's Walk! series of guide books. Walking Route and GPS Waypoints are then drawn onto the map section to produce the map illustrating the detailed walk description.

Walk! Exmoor map sections are sufficient to follow the detailed walk descriptions, but for planning your adventures in this region, and if you wish to divert from the walking routes, we strongly recommend that you purchase the latest OS Explorer maps.

Walking route ·················· , placed alongside the OS map feature

Alternative Route ··················

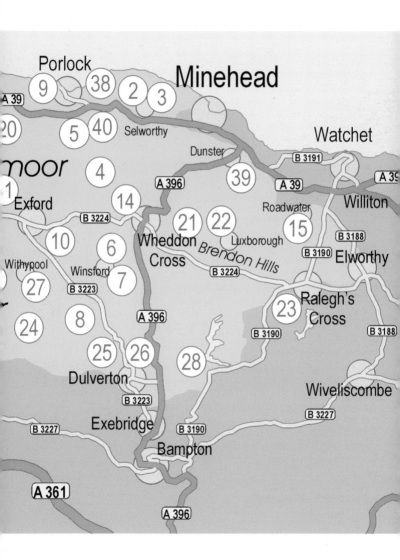

The GPS Waypoint lists in this book (Pages 146-150) are as recorded by David & Carol Hitt while researching the detailed walk descriptions. Waypoint symbols are numbered so that they can be directly identified with the walk description and Waypoint list. All GPS Waypoints are subject to the accuracy of GPS units in the particular location of each Waypoint. GPS reception is good for the majority of the routes; only in the deep *combes* are you likely to be out of reliable GPS reception (see P.146).

Satellite Reception

Accurate location fixes for your GPS unit depend upon receiving signals from four or more satellites. Providing you have good batteries, and that you wait until your GPS has full 'satellite acquisition' before starting out, your GPS will perform well on Exmoor. Where poor satellite reception occurs it is mentioned in the walk description.

Manually Inputting Waypoints

GPS Waypoints are quoted for the OSGB (Ordnance Survey Great Britain) datum and BNG (British National Grid) co-ordinates, making them identical with the OS grid co-ordinates of the position they refer to. To manually input the Waypoints into your GPS we suggest that you:

- switch on your GPS and select 'simulator/standby' mode
- check that your GPS is set to the OSGB datum and BNG 'location/position format'
- input the GPS Waypoints into a 'route' with the same number as the walking route; then when you call up the 'route' on Exmoor there will be no confusion as to which walking route it refers
- repeat the inputting of Waypoints into routes until you have covered all the routes you plan to walk, or until you have used up the memory capacity of your GPS
- turn off your GPS. When you turn your GPS back on, it should return to its normal navigation mode

Note that GPS Waypoints complement the routes in Walk! Exmoor, and are not intended as an alternative to the detailed walking route descriptions.

Personal Navigator Files (PNFs) CD version 3.01

Edited versions of David & Carol's original GPS research tracks and Waypoints are available as downloadable files on our PNFs CD, which also includes all the edited GPS tracks and Waypoints for all the Walk!/Walks guide books published by DWG along with GPS Utility Special Edition software. See DWG websites for more information:

www.walking.demon.co.uk & www.dwgwalking.co.uk

GPS The Easy Way (£4.99)

If you are confused by talk of GPS, but are interested in how this modern navigational aid could enhance your walking enjoyment, then simply seek out a copy of GPS The Easy Way, the UK's best selling GPS manual.

Carol is wearing … David is dressed ... by accident rather than design! Seriously, leaving aside the haute couture catwalks of Milan, fashion's not the issue; comfort, safety and preparation are the main considerations.

- Karrimor **day sacks** 30L and 15L. David's has waist pockets, useful for easy access to frequently needed items.
- David - Loveson's leather **boots** - "well worn, falling apart but can't bear to part with them". Carol - Wainwright lightweight Gore-Tex boots.
- Carol uses 2 **walking poles**, excellent to support knee and back joints, David uses 1 to fend off inquisitive livestock.
- **Water** - as much as we can carry, **sandwiches, fruit & nut cereal bars**, and in winter a small flask of **hot tea**; just a mouthful tastes like nectar.
- **Essential First Aid Kit** including **antiseptic cream** and **wipes**, **plasters, crêpe bandage, insect bite zapper pen** and tweezers.
- **Emergency Pack** consisting of **space blanket, whistle, glucose tablets, torch, spare batteries, loose change** and a bar of **Kendal mint cake** (now well past its sell-by date).
- **GPS**, Silva **compass**, and OS Explorer **map** OL9; printed both sides, it covers the whole of Exmoor.
- Rohan **trousers**, fleece lined Craghopper winter trousers, waterproof over trousers, **gaiters** in winter and wet weather. **Layers** work for us - wicking **T-shirts**, long sleeved **shirts**, Rohan & Sprayway **fleeces**. **Jackets** - Lowe Alpine & Jack Wolfskin - lightweight Keela for summer. Hats - summer **legionnaire's cap** and David's beloved **Tilley hat** (possibly lurking north of Woodbarrow Gate, if anyone comes across it, please return to owner). **Fleece lined caps** complete with Biggles style earflaps - definitely not a fashion statement but indispensable during winter on moors and cliffs. Polartec **head band, gloves**.
- **Mobile phones** - one each in case we get separated, small walking **towel**, drywash **cleansing gel**, Gelert folding **seating pads** - essential to keep posteriors dry, **sunscreen** block, **tissues, loo roll**, lightweight **binoculars, digital camera, lip salve, comb**, mango mania **lip-gloss** (you never know who you'll see in the pub!)

Basic safety considerations, whatever the weather when you start off: -
- Wear appropriate clothing and footwear and carry the right equipment.
- Take frequent drinks of water.
- Stay on route and if in any doubt retrace your steps.
- Let someone know where you intend to walk and estimated return time.
- Know how to use a compass and GPS and carry it on moorland walks.
- Carry a map and guide book.
- On the coast, keep to the paths and stay away from cliff edges.
- In an **Emergency** phone 999 or 112 from a mobile phone or landline for Police/Ambulance/Fire/Coastguard services.

Warmer, wetter weather has encouraged the increase of **ticks** in the countryside. Simple precautions include wearing long trousers tucked into socks and a long sleeved shirt, in light colours (easier to spot ticks and brush them off). If bitten, remove by grasping close to the skin with tweezers and twisting anti-clockwise. Early symptoms may feel like flu. Easily treatable with antibiotics, the earlier it is diagnosed the better, so it's advisable to seek medical assistance.

Respect, Protect and Enjoy the countryside; there's more information about the Countryside Code at www.countrysideaccess.gov.uk

Weather

Mist and fog can descend very quickly on the moors so it's best to get a local forecast beforehand.

On line from www.bbc.co.uk/weather/ukweather/southwest

Meteorological Office Weathercall for Somerset Tel: 09068 505305

1 HUNTER'S INN & WOODY BAY

This route introduces us to splendid walking on Exmoor's rugged coast; a landscape of precipitous cliffs, rocky headlands, *hanging oak woods* and hidden bays. Yet our route is neither steep nor difficult as we use a broad carriageway to steadily climb from **Heddon Valley** high onto heather clad slopes; past a Roman look out point, then along cliff tops with great views to the evocatively named **Woody Bay**. Our return along a beautiful stretch of the **South West Coast Path** offers excellent walking and includes a high waterfall and views over **Heddon's Mouth**, a reputed haunt of smugglers.

3	2.4 H	6¾ miles/11km	340m / 340m	↻	2*

* **Hunter's Inn**; food available all day.

> **Stroll**
> A l o n g   t h e carriageway to the sea cliffs above **Heddon's Mouth** and return the same way (2½ miles/4km).

Detour down to **Woody Bay** beach from Wp.7; ½ mile each way, 25M.

Access by car: from A39 between **Parracombe** and **Lynton** signposted **Heddon's Mouth** and **Hunter's Inn** (SS655482). Park on the road near **Hunter's Inn** or in National Trust car park beside shop and toilets.

From the National Trust Shop (Wp.1 0M) we stroll towards **Hunter's Inn**, bearing right up the road then immediately left onto the 'Woody Bay' path, keeping right at the first junction (Wp.2 3M) on a broad woodland track. An even gradient quickly allows us to strike up a rhythm as we climb above the tree line into a grey green landscape of scree and bracken, enlivened by bright splashes of heather and gorse.

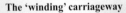

The 'winding' carriageway

Swinging right, we can appreciate the skilfully engineered 19th century carriageway as it bears left around **Hill Brook** before reaching the cliff tops. Horse drawn coaches transported visitors on what must have been an exhilarating if hair-raising journey from **Lynton** to **Hunter's Inn**; now used only by hikers, this wonderful trail offers us a more relaxed means of travel.

Curving right high above **Heddons Mouth**, the gradient eases as we head E along the cliff tops to a 'Roman Fortlet' signpost (Wp.3 31M) for a short detour to admire far reaching views both inland and seaward to **Wales**. It's not surprising that the Romans constructed a look out post on this isolated vantage point (Wp.4 35M 247 metres) in the first century, to keep a watchful eye on the marauding Silures. Today, for us at least, the atmosphere is still conducive to playing at soldiers marching around the low circular ramparts.

Retracing our steps to Wp.3 (39M), we stride out along the winding carriageway as superb views open up ahead along the coast to **Woody Bay**,

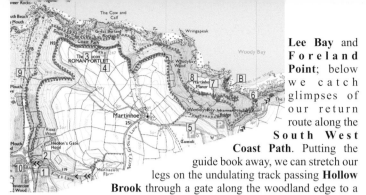

Lee Bay and **Foreland Point**; below we catch glimpses of our return route along the **South West Coast Path**. Putting the guide book away, we can stretch our legs on the undulating track passing **Hollow Brook** through a gate along the woodland edge to a second gate (Wp.5 63M) where we join a road. Walking straight on down the twisting lane between moss covered walls and bluebell covered slopes past **Woody Bay Hotel**, (Wp.6 73M) we turn left through a gate onto the acorn-marked 'Coast Path'. Dropping between *western (hanging) oak woods*, a Site of Special Scientific Interest, to a path junction (Wp.7 82M) we bear left for 'Heddon's Mouth', definitely ignoring the directions on the quirky signpost overhead, otherwise you really would get lost!

Climbing a rough tarmac track we bear right at a gate (Wp.8 87M) onto the 'Hunter's Inn' coast path, wending up through the trees over our only stile, to emerge onto open sea slopes at **Wringapeak** where our route curves left towards the sound of rushing water. **Hollow Brook** waterfall consists of a series of cascades dropping 200 metres down the cliff face and could be considered to be the highest waterfall in the West Country. Our route winds along the cliff slopes gradually ascending a colourful landscape of western gorse, bell heather and ling, around rocky promontories with wonderful views back to **Lee Bay** and **Foreland Point**.

Rounding another headland our downhill path stretches out ahead to **Highveer Point** above **Heddon's Mouth** where we have a helicopter view of the beach and valley below. Leaving the rugged cliffs we turn inland, taking care over a short section of scree, then tramping down the well trodden narrow path towards a dense canopy of trees below. At a path junction (Wp.9 129M) we turn left for 'Hunter's Inn' then straight on past the stone bridge, ignoring the coast path sign, along a meandering path beside the **River Heddon** to our start point (Wp.10 141M).

Woody Bay detour 25M

Woody Bay

It's a half mile walk down to the quiet rock strewn bay; our final descent is on a cobbled path beside a restored lime kiln built into the cliff face. Surrounded by trees clinging to precipitous slopes, this is a great place to picnic and explore rock pools. Affected by earth movements and erosion, jagged rock strata point seaward at acute angles and a waterfall plunges out of a *hanging valley* onto the beach. We retrace our steps for the climb to Wp.7.

2 SELWORTHY, BOSSINGTON & ALLERFORD

The charming villages of **Selworthy**, **Bossington** and **Allerford** lie close together in **Porlock Vale** forming part of the extensive **Holnicote Estate** owned by the National Trust; despite their proximity each has its own distinctive character. Our route captures the essence of a landscape of high heath and cliffs, ancient woodland and chocolate box villages. In early summer the muted tones of wild foxgloves and sea thrift contrast with stronger hues of neatly cultivated traditional cottage-gardens.

Our outward route climbs a wooded *combe* then crosses the open spaces of **Selworthy Beacon** and **Bossington Hill**, offering terrific views across **Porlock Bay**, before a steep adventurous descent beside the cliff edge to **Hurlstone Point**. A more tranquil low level meandering return takes us inland through the three delightful villages and back along the edge of **Porlock Vale**.

| 3 | 2¾ H | 7 miles/11¼km | ⋀⋀ | ↗385m ↘385m | ⚠ * | ↻ | 🍴 3 ** |

* **Adventurous Route**   ** seasonal **Bossington, Allerford, Selworthy Green**

Access by car: Selworthy Church (SS920467) lies ½ mile north of the A39 between **Minehead** and **Lynmouth**. Park in front of the church or in the overflow car park.

Access by bus:
First bus routes Nº38 and Nº300 stop at **Selworthy Turn** on A39.

Extension
This walk can be combined with Walk 3 for a 10 mile/ 16 km walk. Follow Walk 3 to Wp.10 to join Walk 2 at Wp.6.

From the car park we stroll back along the lane in front of **Selworthy Church** to the War Memorial (Wp.1 0M), turning right through the gate onto the 'Selworthy Beacon' bridleway, keeping the stream on our left for an easy ascent along the wooded valley. Going straight on at the first 'Selworthy Beacon' fingerpost to a fork, (Wp.2 7M) we take the 'Selworthy Combe' right hand track along a glade to bear left then right onto heath land (Wp.3 13M).

The fingerpost at Wp.4

Crunching up a steep section of stony track we come to a path intersection where a blue tipped 'Selworthy Beacon' fingerpost (Wp.4 21M) points us left onto an easier gradient, giving us time to pause and admire views over **Selworthy Combe**, **Horner** and onward to **Dunkery Beacon** on the southern horizon.

Following 'Selworthy Beacon' signs we fork left, then bear left on the road for

200 yards to a bend, taking the first wide track on the right (Wp.5 28M) for an easy stroll (W) to the cairn and vantage point (308 metres). Here deep inland wooded valleys merge into coastal views and over the expanse of the **Bristol Channel** to South Wales; on a hot summer's day, it's easy to while away an hour watching tiny turquoise butterflies flick between gorse while skylarks sing overhead.

From the summit we stride out (W) along a wide stony track on a gradual downhill route to a junction, (Wp.6 40M) heading straight on following the acorn symbols and 'Coast path' signs to a fork (Wp.7 47M) where we bear right (NW) for 'Bossington'. Our track ahead resembles an enormous snake squirming across the heath towards increasingly dominant views of **Porlock Bay** with its backdrop of cliffs. Passing another 'coast path Bossington' sign we reach the top of **Hurlstone Combe** and a path junction beside a bench (Wp.8 59M) where we have a choice of routes.

Easier option
The official coast path signposted 'Footpath to Porlock' falls steeply between **Hurlstone Combe's** concave slopes to Wp.11 and should definitely be taken in poor weather, or if walkers suffer from vertigo.

Main (Adventurous) Route
For adventurous hikers, we turn right beside the bench onto a narrow path for a challenging descent around the cliff edge to **Hurlstone Point**, passing a warning sign advising us 'to take extreme care, the path is extremely narrow and exposed especially in bad weather conditions'.

Skirting the top of the *combe* along the hillside we head towards an outcrop on the cliff edge, turning left 50 yards beforehand on a small gravel path to drop around the side of the rocks.

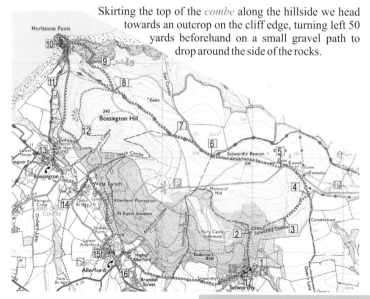

On the steep, exposed path

Treading carefully down this steep exposed path across a short section of bare rock, we then turn sharp right (Wp.9 68M) for a skittering zigzag descent beneath the sheer cliff face; making slow progress we have time to stop and take in stunning views over **Porlock Bay's** marsh and pebble beach 150 metres below.

After the scree our path levels out, passing the derelict lookout at **Hurlstone Point** (Wp.10 81M); heading inland we fork left to a path intersection at the foot of **Hurlstone Combe**, going straight on for 'Allerford' (Wp.11 85M). Clear easy walking (S) along a bracken covered slope brings us to the stone boundary wall of ancient woodland; turning right downhill for 'Bossington' (Wp.12 98M) to a path junction, we go left on the 'Coast path' across a footbridge to a red telephone box (Wp.13 106M). Our route turns left between **Bossington's** stone cottages; their distinctive semi circular bread ovens protruding into well kept gardens. Ambling along this pleasant village lane, and for us at least resisting more than one cream tea, we cross the village green past the **Falconry Centre** towards **Allerford**.

Just beyond the **Medieval Chapel of Ease** we go left over the stone bridge beside **Lynch Country House** (Wp.14 113M) signed 'Public bridleway Selworthy Beacon'; the tarmac becomes a path as we climb between houses into a wood, turning right on a footpath for 'Allerford & Selworthy'. After a gentle climb we bear right for 'Allerford' on either the higher or lower path, crossing the river on a footbridge to reach the road (Wp.15 128M).

Bearing left into **Allerford** past the post office and **Rural Life Museum**, we cross the picturesque pack horse bridge on our left, climbing uphill then swinging right along the lane to the cottages on our left (Wp.16 139M).

Allerford

Our route goes straight on along a rough stony track for 'Selworthy', steadily climbing along **Porlock Vale** and after walking through a short wooded section we emerge onto a single file cobbled path to reach farm buildings and thatched cottages at **Selworthy**. Turning left up the lane to the public toilets we enter **Selworthy Green** via a pedestrian gate on our left, following the winding paths in front of the **NT Information Centre** to the War Memorial (Wp.17 157M).

3 SELWORTHY AND NORTH HILL - A PANORAMIC SPLENDOUR

This enjoyable route takes on an added zest and sparkle when the clouds are high and the air is clear, so that from **North Hill** and **Selworthy Beacon** we can absorb breathtaking views in all directions; add a chocolate-box hamlet, a country estate and the site of an ancient settlement and we have all the ingredients for an interesting and visually stimulating walk.

Standing high above **Porlock Vale, Selworthy's** bold lime-washed church marks the start of our main ascent along a wooded *combe* onto open level heath for a relaxing coast path stroll, before we descend through the mature woods of the **Holnicote Estate** past an Iron Age hill fort to idyllic **Selworthy Green**.

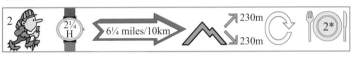

2   2¼H   6¼ miles/10km   230m / 230m   2*

* **Periwinkle Cottage Tearoom** (Mar – Oct)

Access by car: Selworthy Church (SS920467) lies ½ mile north of the A39 between **Minehead** and **Lynmouth**. Park in front of the church or in the overflow car park.

Access by bus:
First bus routes Nº38 and Nº300 stop at **Selworthy Turn** on A39.

Extension
This walk can be combined with Walk 2 for a 10 mile/16 km walk (ascents & descents 425 metres). Follow Walk 3 to Wp.10 to join Walk 2 at Wp.6

Selworthy Church

Our route from **Selworthy Church** heads left down the lane to the War Memorial (Wp.1 0M) swinging right through a gate onto the 'Selworthy Beacon' bridleway and steadily climbing above the valley stream through mature woodland.

Going straight on at the first 'Selworthy Beacon' fingerpost to a fork, (Wp.2 7M) we take the right hand 'Selworthy Combe' track wending the length of a delightful glade to bear left then right (Wp.3 13M). As trees give way to heath we climb steeply up the hillside across a path junction (Wp.4 21M) signed 'North Hill' to the hilltop and where a track joins from the left we curve right along a comfortable level path between high gorse bushes. Gradually views open up inland to Exmoor, ahead to the **Quantock Hills** and when joining the road (Wp.5 30M) we can see across the **Bristol Channel** to **Wales**.

Turning right to a cattle grid, we cross diagonally left in front of it through a pedestrian gate (Wp.6 34M) strolling parallel to the road (E) along the grassy

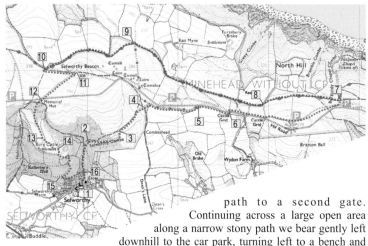

path to a second gate. Continuing across a large open area along a narrow stony path we bear gently left downhill to the car park, turning left to a bench and signpost (Wp.7 51M). Splendid views stretch in front along the **North Somerset** coast including the town of **Watchet** where the **Quantocks** come down to the sea.

Now, our route for 'Bossington' goes left (W) beside **North Hill** on a level section of the acorn marked coast path and depending on our mood and the season, we either bowl along in the crisp autumn air or saunter in the summer sunshine.

Ignoring the next signpost marked 'Alternative Rugged Coast Path', we stride to a gate (Wp.8 62M) past grazing Exmoor ponies to re-enter the **Holnicote Estate** then on through a second gate near the steeply wooded **Bramble Combe**. Stepping out between heath and fields our easy track passes a tarmac lane (Wp.9 82M), continuing until the trail reaches a T-junction (Wp.10 95M).

Leaving the coast path we turn left uphill to the trig point and cairn at **Selworthy Beacon** (Wp.11 100M 308 metres) to be greeted with a stunning 360 degree panorama; west to the rugged **North Devon** and **Somerset** coast, south to **Dunkery Beacon** and on a clear day the **Brecon Beacons** can be seen to the north.

Swinging right down the broad path (SW) across the road (Wp.12 108M) we bear right into the group of large pine trees to the aptly named 'wind and weather hut' erected in memory of Sir Thomas Dyke Acland (who died in 1871) who planted several areas of woodland on these slopes to mark the birth of his nine children.

The wind and weather hut

Strolling past the hut, we fork immediately left down a curving grass track through a lightly wooded area into a clearing; keeping left where the tracks divide (Wp.13 114M), we arrive at the perimeter ditch and earth ramparts of **Bury Castle Ancient Settlement** (Wp.14 117M). This is a delightful spot for a break to enjoy views of the **Quantocks** and imagine what it must have been like for Iron Age man to have eked out an existence centuries ago.

Turning right downhill beside the ditch for 80 yards, we keep left beside the stone wall to the 'Bury Castle' sign, then right through the gate, beyond which our path zigzags down through the trees bearing left onto a bridleway to a T junction (Wp.15 126M).

Going left to 'Selworthy' our track narrows before we go through a gate towards the footbridge, (Wp.16 130M) turning right immediately before the stream through another gate. Keeping the stream on our left, it is a few steps to the picturesque setting of **Selworthy Green** where we can wander between the cream and brown thatched cottages before returning in front of the NT Information Centre to the War Memorial (Wp.1 135M).

Selworthy Green's medieval cob and stone buildings were redesigned in 1828 by Sir Thomas Dyke Acland for his estate pensioners. At the quaintly named **Periwinkle Cottage Tearooms** we've the difficult task of choosing which home-made snack or cake to devour with a pot of tea; look out for floral tea cosies and tame birds hoovering up crumbs from outside tables!

Selworthy Green

4 STOKE PERO COMMON & DUNKERY BEACON

It's always satisfying to scale new heights and blow the cobwebs away; whether battered by invigorating westerlies, or embraced by gentle breezes, this moorland route to Exmoor's highest point **Dunkery Beacon** fits the bill perfectly.

Starting from **Stoke Pero Common**, we cross a wide expanse of Access Land on **Dunkery Beacon**'s northern slopes before a stiff climb to the summit and a wonderful panorama of northern Exmoor and the coast. A level track takes us west along a broad ridge to **Rowbarrow** cairns and down to **Lang Combe Head**; after descending to a road we swing down a path into the secluded woodland setting of **Stoke Combe**, crossing three delightful streams, before climbing over a common to complete this lovely walk. A GPS or compass should be carried in case of poor weather and for the best views this is preferably a walk for fine days.

| 2 | 2H | 5.7 miles/9.2km | ⌃⌃ | 285m / 285m | ↻ | 🍴 0 |

| **Stroll** |
| To **Dunkery Beacon**: take the **Wheddon Cross** to **Horner** road, park in the lay-bys on **Dunkery Hill** (SS 903418) and walk along a broad track WSW to the cairn. |

| **Shorter Walk** |
| (4.1 miles/6.6km, ascents & descents 220 metres) Turn right down the road at Wp.5. |

Access by car: The start point (SS 870427) is 4 miles north of **Exford**. Follow **Porlock** signs, then fork right for **Cloutsham** at **Hillhead Cross** and **Porlock Post**. Going downhill across the moor look for a line of fir trees on the left; **Dicky's Path** is just before, on the right. Park off road on the wider grass verges.

The sign at Wp.1

A roadside log barrier and a sign for 'Dicky's Path to Webber's Post' (Wp.1 0M) marks our start point as we head off down a track into a small valley, crossing a stream and swinging sharp left up a bracken covered slope. Deer may be seen grazing in fields on our left, or deftly jinking through the heather and bracken covering the sweeping northern slopes of **Dunkery Hill**; on top we can just make out its stone cairn. Our track levels out beside a row of beech trees, running along the contours before bending right down into a *combe*; stepping over or through a stream, depending on the amount of tumbling water, we climb up to follow a long row of large beech trees.

As our path gradually descends we have our first views of **Bossington Hill**, the ridge to **Selworthy Beacon** and glimpses of the **Bristol Channel**.

Curving gently left and continuing over a brow past two circular wire enclosures, we reach a path crossroads overlooking **Aller Combe** (Wp.2 23M); there are views to our left of **Cloutsham Farm** with its Tyrolean façade. Turning right up a steep grass path, we head slowly towards **Dunkery Beacon**; the half-mile ascent could be a boring slog were it not for the views over **Porlock Vale** which become increasingly grand each time we stop to regain our breath.

Views over Porlock Vale

The time to the next waypoint includes all our frequent breathers, giving an indication of how long this climb takes; and unable to see the Beacon above, it's a voyage into the unknown! Eventually, our path through the heather briefly flattens before we tackle a short even steeper section, suddenly arriving at the summit and cairn (Wp.3 47M 519m).

Now our ascent becomes worthwhile as the panorama includes the coast to the **Quantocks**, inland to the **Brendon Hills** and across rolling moors; a circular viewpoint finder points to the main landscape features. Conservation work has been carried out by the National Trust to protect the adjacent cairns for future generations. Having completed our main climb and taking a well deserved rest, we turn right beside the cairn, strolling along the right hand of two paths running west along a ridge.

Our clear stony track descends a little way before we gradually regain height, heading for the small stone cairn of **Little Rowbarrow** a mile ahead on the horizon; passing it, we soon curve right at **Great Rowbarrow** (Wp.4 69M) where a sign tells us that these Bronze Age burial mounds are some 3500-4000 years old.

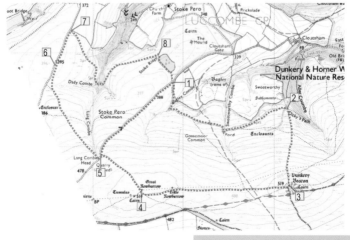

Tramping steadily downhill (NW) with views over **Porlock Bay**, we arrive at a small car park beside a road (Wp.5 76M); for the shorter walk turn right down the road to the start. Our route goes left up the road for 25 yards to the head of a deep ravine on our right and bears right over a stream through heather along the top left edge; when the deep valley swings away north we go straight on downhill (NW), bending slightly right before our grassy path peters out and we step onto a road (Wp.6 91M).

Stoke Combe

Going right along the road to a field bank and metal gate (Wp.7 97M), we turn right back onto the moor, taking the more distinct right hand track, away from the bank.

Walking downhill, the densely wooded steep slopes of **Stoke Combe** suddenly appear in front; as our path reaches the tree line we swing right, down a hillside to a valley floor, crossing two small streams before bearing left over a third. This is a pleasant secluded spot to relax and picnic; the combining streams pour into **Horner Water** which eventually flows into the **Bristol Channel** at **Bossington**.

Having steadily climbed a clear track onto a level heather moor, we turn right at a path crossroads (Wp.8 117M) in front of a line of fir trees; walking between tussock grass towards final views of the cairn high on **Dunkery Beacon**, our path bears right to the road opposite our start point (Wp.9 121M).

Dunkery Hill
Dunkery Hill is part of the Holnicote Estate which has been managed by the National Trust since 1935; a plaque on top of **Dunkery Beacon** commemorates the hand over by the Acland family and other landowners.

Much of the area is Access Land comprising moors and deep wooded valleys; a number of criss-crossing paths were given names by the Acland family including 'Dicky's Path'. Due to visitor numbers, two cairns either side of the Beacon have been covered with river gravel and planted with heathers to preserve this Scheduled Ancient Monument for future generations.

5 HORNER, STOKE PERO & WEBBER'S POST

The main part of this walk is through ancient *sessile oak woods* along hillsides and beside fast flowing streams; timber has always played a significant role on Exmoor, being cultivated for tanning, burnt for charcoal and used as building material. We visit a tiny moorland church at **Stoke Pero** to see how donkey power helped to build the splendid curved roof; later, we view a modern celebration of woodcraft at **Webber's Post** where a collection of wood sculptures is set in natural surroundings around an easy access trail.

Our sheltered route runs on clearly signed paths up **Horner Water** and **Stoke Combe** to **Stoke Pero** and along a hillside to **Cloutsham Ball**; after dropping steeply into **East Water** and ascending to **Webber's Post**, our final woodland stroll is downhill to **Horner**. In the spirit of adventurous walking we should mention that during a three-quarter mile section up **Stoke Combe** it's necessary to ford the stream a dozen times; not normally a problem, but after prolonged rain be prepared to get your boots wet - fortunately an alternative drier way is available!

3   2½ H   6.9 miles/11.1km   360m / 360m   1*

* Seasonal tearooms **Horner**

Shorter Walk
After 20 minutes turn left over two footbridges along **East Water** valley floor to Wp.14, then left up 'Priestway' (2½ miles/4km, ascents & descents 170 metres).

Alternative drier route
At Wp.4 turn left uphill to Wp.8 and right to **Stoke Pero Church**.

Access by car: **Horner** car park (SS 898456) is 1 mile south of **Red Post** junction between **Porlock** and **Allerford** on A39.

Horner Water

Turning left along a lane from the main car park exit (Wp.1 0M) we bear right into 'Horner Woods' at a grass triangle, crossing a bridge and going through a gate; keeping **Horner Water** on our left, it's a pleasant stroll up the valley on a well-trodden stony track.

The ancient *sessile oak woods* form part of the Access Land in this area and are popular with hikers and horse riders alike; once managed for charcoal production and coppiced on a regular basis, they are now owned by the National Trust and left to regenerate naturally.

After 20 minutes, ignoring a footbridge on our left, our track runs along a bank above the river; as it starts to rise to the right, we fork left on a narrower path (Wp.2 22M) staying beside the water.

Bearing left, our broader path (Wp.3 28M) continues up the valley to a footbridge and path crossroads (Wp.4 38M), (for the alternative drier route go left signed 'Granny's Ride Stoke Pero'); we go straight on keeping the river on our left through woodland glades to a 'Stoke Combe' sign (Wp.5 45M). Crossing a footbridge, and ignoring a right hand bank path, we bear slightly left away from the water; heading uphill for a short distance our path forks left, descending into a narrower valley alongside a stream.

Now we put the book away to concentrate on a fording escapade; the path and watercourse twist and turn in opposite directions, so we spend the next 20 minutes repeatedly criss-crossing the stream - we counted 12! After heavy rain this section requires concentration, though an alternative route starts from Wp.4; see the information box after the introduction. Eventually gaining height above the stream, we arrive at a road (Wp.6 64M) and turn left to climb steeply to the tree line, then on to **Church Farm** and **Stoke Pero Church**; our route turns left in front of the farm (Wp.7 73M) along the blue-marked 'Priestway', but it's worth a detour to the church.

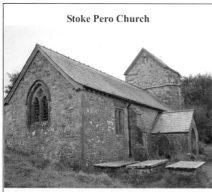

Stoke Pero Church

Stoke Pero is the highest and most remote church on Exmoor, with a medieval porch and tower dating from 13th century; major restoration in 1897 was funded by Sir Thomas Acland. A sketch inside the church depicts Zulu the donkey, who pulled a cart twice daily from **Porlock** carrying oak timbers to construct the impressive wagon roof.

Continuing along a short section of enclosed track then across the foot of a field, a small 'Priestway' sign points us left through a gate down a woodland path; keeping right at a fork marked with a double headed arrow (Wp.8 80M), we stride out near the woodland edge to a second path fork (Wp.9 85M) where a blue arrow on a fence post points us left on a narrower downhill path.

Ignoring paths on either side, we continue straight on over a stream (Wp.10 89M) curving left up a slope, with glimpses across **Horner Valley** then descend around another *combe*. Regaining height we swing out of the wood onto a bracken and gorse covered hilltop, bearing left at a path junction (Wp.11 103M) on the 'Priestway'; there is a well-positioned bench under a fir tree from which views of **Porlock Vale** can be admired.

Approaching Cloutsham Ball

Heading on and ignoring right and left paths, we reach a view point at **Cloutsham Ball** above **East Water** (Wp.12 107M); to our right is the smooth

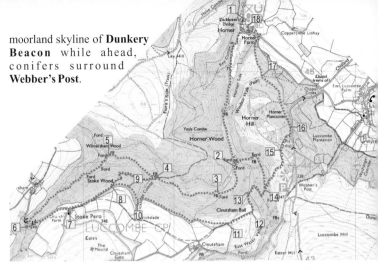

moorland skyline of **Dunkery Beacon** while ahead, conifers surround **Webber's Post**.

Going sharp left downhill into silver birches, we bear right at a path T-junction and right again after a few yards (Wp.13 110M) on a track that drops steeply down to a stream; crossing a footbridge, we go left to a signpost, taking the right-hand 'Priestway' (Wp.14 117M) up a hillside path to a junction with **Webber's Post Easy Access Trail** (Wp.15 130M).

The enigmatic frog

Arranged around the short trail is a sculpture exhibition created in 2004 from local timbers by a group of international artists; it's only a short circular detour to appreciate the variety of design and quality of craftsmanship - our favourites are the apple and enigmatic frog.

Going straight on through gorse and bracken our 'Bridleway' descends to a road, (Wp.16 134M) where we turn left for 30 yards then left again on 'His Honour's Path to Horner'. Now our straight path runs gently downhill through a wood across several track intersections, including one which indicates that we've come from **Chapel Steep** (Wp.17 143M).

Going straight on and eventually descending a steep stony section, we go through a high deer gate on our left. Turning left on a road past a mill to **Horner Tea Gardens** the car park path is on our right (Wp.18 154M).

6 WINSFORD, WINSFORD HILL, & THE PUNCHBOWL

The attractive village of **Winsford**, mentioned in the Domesday Book, has considerable character and rural charm; a notable feature being the criss-cross of packhorse bridges and narrow lanes over the **River Exe** and **Winn Brook**. Thoughts of the quaint thatched pub and tea room awaiting our return, spur us on as we leave the village green to climb a bridleway onto the moor.

Far reaching views accompany us as we stroll past the **Caractacus Stone** to the summit of **Winsford Hill** where a splendid panorama extends way beyond Exmoor. Skirting around the extraordinary **Punch Bowl** our return pastoral stroll is along the side of a valley.

A plaque commemorating one of **Winsford**'s eminent sons can be seen on a house opposite the Post Office; this was the birthplace of Ernest Bevin, Minister of Labour during World War II and later Foreign Secretary.

Access by car: **Winsford** (SS 906349) lies 2 miles west of A396 **Dunster-Tiverton** road, 5 miles south of **Wheddon Cross**.
Access by bus: DevonBus Nº398 **Tiverton-Minehead**; restricted services go via **Winsford**

Winsford Hill Bridleway

Starting at the War Memorial (Wp.1 0M) and village green we walk past **The Royal Oak** up a lane to the bridleway for 'Winsford Hill', turning left beside a stone wall (Wp.2 4M) onto a track that soon becomes a sunken lane running between hedges and fields. Climbing gradually at first, then more steeply, we pick our way over bedrock, with views over **Winsford,** before swinging right over the brow to descend along the side of a valley through a gate (Wp.3 18M).

Going left, then right over a stile and footbridge, our 'Summerway' bridleway climbs through conifers beside the right hand stream and beech trees before bearing right onto a wider forest track (Wp.4 25M).

Slogging up a short shaley track and having thankfully completed our main climb, we emerge from the wood and turn right through a gate (Wp.5 32M); keeping along the field edge and ignoring the first pedestrian gate in the far right hand corner we go through a second gate 50 yards further on (Wp.6 36M).

Taking the left hand fork away from the hedge onto the moor, it's a comfortable stroll (NW) to the top of the common, known as 'the allotment',

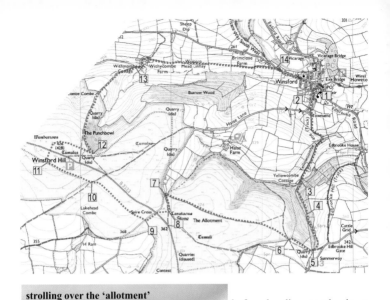

strolling over the 'allotment'

before heading gently down through a gate (Wp.7 56M) just to the left of a grey roofed house. The vista to our right is typical of Exmoor's scenic variety; an undulating patchwork quilt of fields topped with open moors and wide horizons.

Turning immediately left beside the bank, a narrow path leads us to a stone shelter (Wp.8 58M) which protects the ancient **Caractacus Stone**, inscribed 'Carataci Nepus' (kinsman of Caractacus), possibly a memorial for a descendant of King Caractacus. Turning right, away from the bank along a short path to **Spire Cross**, a traditional signpost directs us towards 'Knaplock'; carefully crossing the road we go along the lane for 175 yards, then turn right up a broad grass track (Wp.9 62M).

The Caractacus Stone

Steadily ascending through heather and gorse, views of the **Barle Valley** open up to the left as our route levels out to cross a track junction (Wp.10 72M); we continue straight on up the right hand track to the brow of the hill. Turning right up a narrow path (Wp.11 81M) across a road to the summit of **Winsford**

Hill (426 metres) and the **Wambarrows** *tumuli* we are greeted with an absolutely magnificent 360 degree panorama. While resisting the temptation to get carried away with superlatives, the views from here are the best on southern Exmoor; on a clear day we can see the **Blackdown Hills** and **East Devon**, **Dartmoor**'s eastern profile, and a long stretch of the **North Devon** coast, **Bristol Channel** and **Wales**.

Bearing right from the trig point our path joins a broader track; striding downhill, (ESE) and ignoring the first left hand path, we reach a track junction and bear left along the rim of the **Punch Bowl** (Wp.12 90M).

View from the rim of the 'Punch Bowl'

This huge amphitheatre is an unusual natural phenomenon, the cause of which is still debated; some geological research suggests it may have been formed by glacial activity. An alternative, highly improbable legend is that the Devil scooped out earth, flinging it away to form **Dunkery Beacon**! The depression becomes more pronounced as we descend a wide grassy path, leaving the moor to enter fields above **Withycombe Farm**. Following blue marks beside a right hand fence, we go right through a gate for 'Withycombe', then left as our dirt track swings gradually down to a gate (Wp.13 107M).

Going right through the gate down the track, we double back over a bridge and through the farmyard; the signpost points us right up the track through a gate, then immediately right on a yellow-marked 'Winsford' path. Our route now runs (E) beside right hand hedge banks as we potter through gates and fields along the side of the **Winn Brook Valley** heading towards **Winsford** church. After 20 minutes we enter a narrow path climbing over three stiles to join **Ash Lane** (Wp.14 130M) and turn right downhill for **Winsford**. At **Sunnymead**, the white house with a bowed roof, we turn right down a path, crossing a tiny packhorse bridge to the **Royal Oak** for a final turn around the green to the War Memorial (Wp.15 138M).

7 WINSFORD CIRCULAR via BYE COMMON & THE EXE VALLEY

Winsford is a lovely small village set in an idyllic spot in the **Exe Valley** just below the moorland edge. Its thatched pub and tea room set round a green with two small streams flowing beneath tiny bridges make it an excellent place to start and end this gem of a walk.

There are some walks which suddenly surprise you and transport you into a quite unexpected world. Soon after our start, when we leave the lane it's a bit like clambering through the back of the wardrobe into the Land of Narnia. This different pastoral world we enter is one of peace, quiet solitude and unspoiled scenic beauty - no roads, just paths and tracks.

Our outward route climbs to a high path with absolutely wonderful views of the steep sided valley and a distant moorland panorama while our gentle return is beside a lovely river.

This walk can be enjoyed at any time of the year, but it does suit a warm sunny day when you have plenty of time to sit and enjoy the splendid natural beauty of the surroundings. An added plus is that there are no stiles just gateways!

2	1H 50M * 5¼ miles/8.4km 220m / 220m 3

* plus ½ hour for the alternative finish

Access by car: Winsford (SS 906349) lies 2 miles west of A396 **Dunster-Tiverton** road, 5 miles south of **Wheddon Cross**.

Access by bus: DevonBus N ° 398 **Tiverton-Minehead**; restricted services go via **Winsford**.

Shorter walk
Turn right at Wp.4, going down the track into the valley and turning right to rejoin the main walk at Wp.8 (3.4 miles/5.4km).

Extension
This walk can be combined with Walk 10 for an 11.3 mile/18.2km figure of eight route along the **Exe Valley** and surrounding hills. Follow Walk 7 to Wp.7, turn left to the bridge and cross right over the river to join Walk 10 at Wp.9 to **Exford** and then back over the hills to the river at **East Nethercote**. Rejoin Walk 7 at Wp.7 for the return to **Winsford**.

Ash Lane, Winsford

We start between the **Bridge Cottage Tearoom** and the War Memorial (Wp.1 0M), heading up **Ash Lane** over a footbridge beside a ford. Passing the art gallery on our left, we climb steadily between small houses and bungalows to the edge of the village and the sign 'Winsford'.

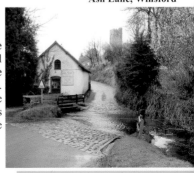

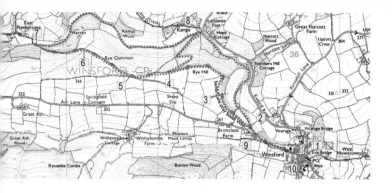

We go through the gate on our right signed 'Exford 4½ miles', and though our path starts off along a short piece of tarmac, suddenly when you least expect it, there we are standing slap bang in the country with a splendid view of the **Exe Valley**.

This is just a taster, for as we gain height the views get better and better. After 200 yards the path divides (Wp.2 9M) and we take the left path signed 'Exford via Bye Common' (NW); our route will eventually return to this point along the other path. As we steadily climb beside a row of mature beech trees there are plenty of gaps to our right giving ever bigger views of the valley, the moorland beyond and back to **Winsford**.

Going through one pedestrian gate and then a second, we turn left for 20 yards to a 'Footpath' signpost pointing right (Wp.3 19M). We're now at the top of the hill, strolling along the tree line to reach two gates where we go right then left. Clear of the trees, our level path runs by the field edge, high above the steep valley sides with magnificent scenery across Exmoor ahead and to our right; the readily identifiable profile of **Dunkery Hill** and its beacon lies along the northern skyline.

A leisurely pace ensures we can absorb the breathtaking views of the **Exe Valley** towards **Curr Cleave** that are truly beautiful in all seasons. Farmhouses and fields nestle into an unspoilt natural landscape of steep, smooth moorland slopes and flat-topped hills. Woods and pastures blend together in a palette of green.

... breathtaking views ...

Passing through a gate our path is joined by a track coming up the hill on our right (Wp.4 31M); the shorter walk turns right down to **Larcombe Wood**. Our route takes us along the hilltop through a gate into a field following a track which soon peters out. We aim for the signpost diagonally right; it can't be missed since it is plonked in the middle of the field next to a standing stone!

(Wp.5 38M); deer may occasionally be seen during this part of our walk. Swinging right (WNW) we follow the 'Bridleway Exford via Nethercote' sign to go across **Bye Common** and then down the track with a post and wire fence on our right to pass through a field gate. On our right we take the second gate (Wp.6 47M), then immediately turn left along the field track beside the hedgebank to pass through another gate.

We are now at the top of a track that will take us down to the valley floor. Our steep descent brings us to the **River Exe** (Wp.7 56M) where we turn right on the level riverside track. Turn left for the extended walk combined with Walk 10.

Depending on the time of year, the river can flow fast and furious or just be a gentle meandering babble. Either way, it's an extremely pleasant route for our return to **Winsford**. Herons flap lazily up the valley and the Dippers with their clean white breasts suddenly catch the eye as they hop from rock to rock and skim the water.

It's an easy 25 minute stroll to **Larcombe Wood** along a level track, following the valley's curves beside the tree lined river banks. The steep, rounded bracken-covered hills that we walked along earlier are high to our right.

We come to the start of the **Larcombe Millennium Wood of Remembrance** where native tree planting is taking place on the valley slopes in aid of local hospices. Our track approaches a bridge (Wp.8 81M) at **Larcombe**; we do not cross the river but bear right through the field gate along a path through rough pasture.

The riverside track (near Wp.8)

Keeping the river on our left we follow an undulating path, muddy after rain, that eventually rises away from the river to **Ash Lane** (Wp.9 103M).

After our final short ascent it's time to step out of one delightful world and return down the lane to the equally enjoyable world of **Winsford** (Wp.10 110M) and the anticipation of a light lunch or fine cream tea at **The Bridge Tea Rooms** or a few yards away across the green the attraction of the thatched **Royal Oak Inn** where bar meals are served at lunchtimes and evenings.

An alternative finish

A short, interesting ½ mile detour takes us to the parish church and across two packhorse bridges. To visit the **Church of St Mary Magdalene** on **The Steep**, walk down **Ash Lane** and look for the second of two finger posts 'Footpath to Church' opposite **Hill View**, in the left hand hedge.

St. Mary Magdalene Church, Winsford

We climb a few steps to turn right into the churchyard. The 11th century Norman church stands proudly above the village with an imposing 90 foot high tower built in three stages. The interior has several interesting architectural features including a Norman font and rounded arch stone doorway; information leaflets are available.

We leave the church and turn left, go through the gates and turn left along a pretty lane and then right round the corner to a long row of white houses. On our left in the hedge is a small footpath that curves down to the river and set in a glade is a narrow moss covered twin arched packhorse bridge for us to cross. As we turn right onto the road we re-cross the river on another bridge and return along the road to the car park.

8 TARR STEPS & WINSFORD HILL

Tarr Steps Clapper Bridge is an historic monument to man's bridge building ingenuity. Popular with visitors, it is set in the lovely peaceful surroundings of the **Barle Valley**. Our route takes us upstream, along a pretty valley through ancient protected woodlands before climbing onto the moorland of **Winsford Hill**; enjoying a wonderful panorama we stride out along Access Land running either side of a ridge. After visiting the unusual **Punch Bowl** and a 5th century inscribed stone, we cross open country onto **Mounsey Hill** before descending to **Tarr Steps**. The Access Land offers alternative paths for shorter routes back to **Tarr Steps.**

3 | 3H | 8.8 miles/14.2km | 330m / 330m | 3*

*Tarr Farm Inn

Access by car: **Tarr Steps** car park (SS 872324) is 1½ miles west of B3223, 6 miles north of **Dulverton** and 8 miles south of **Exford**

Heading down a valley from the 'Scenic Footpath' sign (Wp.1 0M) we pass **Tarr Farm Inn,** crossing the river on a magnificent stone *clapper bridge* to turn immediately

<table>
<tr><td>Stroll</td></tr>
<tr><td>To Wp.3, cross the footbridge and turn right to Tarr Steps. (2.3 miles/3.7 km)</td></tr>
<tr><td>Shorter walk</td></tr>
<tr><td>To Wp.11, Spire Cross, then follow Knaplock lane to Tarr Steps. (6.6 miles/10.6 km, ascents & descents 285 metres)</td></tr>
<tr><td>Extension</td></tr>
<tr><td>To Wp.9, then join Walk 6 from Wp.12 to Winsford. Return on Walk 6 to Wp.8, Caractacus Stone and rejoin Walk 8 to the end. (12.7 miles/20.4 km, ascents & descents 470 metres)</td></tr>
</table>

The stepping stones before Wp.3

right (Wp.2 8M) into **North Barton Wood** along a riverside path. Strolling through this **National Nature Reserve,** a wire contraption spanning the river catches the eye; not a bridge for budding Tarzans, it's designed to catch fallen trees when the **Barle** is in flood. Walking upstream, our path soon climbs giving views of wooded slopes, then drops to an impressive set of stepping stones over a tributary where we turn right onto a footbridge (Wp.3 26M).

Crossing the river, we go left along a twisting path following an undulating route along the bank; taking care as we pick our way over slippery rocks and protruding tree roots. Although unlikely to see the small population of otters and dormice living in this area, birds such as herons and dippers may be seen from the banks. After a stile our path becomes easier as we negotiate a footbridge and gate, swinging onto the river bank before crossing a second footbridge to reach a blue bridleway signpost (Wp.4 46M).

Now following signs for 'Winsford Hill' and bearing right through a gate, our track climbs beside a right hand stream, crossing over a manmade miniature waterfall; after a short sharp ascent we go right through a gate near the valley top, then along a field edge to a lane.

Turning left and trudging steadily uphill, the lane bends left after a cattle grid (Wp.5 62M); here, we go straight on up a track, curving gently left (E) between gorse to a signed path junction (Wp.6 65M). Still gradually climbing towards the B3223 road, we turn right shortly before it at a path crossroads (Wp.7 72M); our gently ascending track (ESE) stays parallel with the road giving good views over the **Barle Valley** and way beyond to **Dartmoor**'s distinctive eastern silhouette.

As our track levels, views open up over **Devon**'s timeless rural landscape; keeping our eyes peeled left for a narrow path through the heather, we go along it (Wp.8 83M), crossing the road to **Winsford Hill** trig point (426 metres). Superb extensive views include **Dunkery Beacon**, a stretch of the **North Devon** coast, and over the **Bristol Channel** to **Wales**. On our left are the three **Wambarrows** *tumuli*, large Bronze Age mounds suggesting that important people were buried here.

Winsford Hill trig point

Going diagonally right from the trig point, our path merges into a broader track; striding downhill (ESE), ignoring left and right hand paths, we arrive at the rim of the dramatic **Punch Bowl** (Wp.9 91M); the origin of this unusual natural phenomenon is open to debate, some form of glacial activity being a possible explanation.

Still following the broad grass track (E) swinging very gently left to a path crossroads (Wp.10 99M), we take a slightly narrower path second on our right (SE), dropping towards a grey roofed house.

Just before a lane, we keep right on the path, wending our way between gorse, crossing the lane between a modern traffic warning sign (Wp.11 109M) and a traditional signpost at **Spire Cross**. The shorter route heads from **Spire Cross** towards **Knaplock**, following a lane back to **Tarr Steps** car park.

Bearing left along a path, we reach a stone hut sheltering the ancient **Caractacus Stone**, thought to be a 5th century memorial for a descendant of King Caractacus; the inscription 'Carataci Nepus' means 'kinsman of Caractacus'.

Keeping right behind the stone hut, we gently climb a track roughly parallel to a hedge bank; then, descending over grass and heath, gradually bear away from the hedge to a track T-junction. Going left on a red earth track, we swing right in front of a hedge for a few yards to a field corner (Wp.12 124M), continuing along a contour path beside field boundaries; there are pleasant pastoral views to our left, beyond which lie the bare slopes of **Haddon Hill**. Our route gradually curves right to a point where the field boundary swings away left; here the path divides (Wp.13 136M) and we fork right (WSW) to the B3223, carefully crossing the road onto a **Tarr Steps** lane.

The Tarr Steps signpost

Immediately beyond a cattle grid (Wp.14 141M) we bear left onto a 'Tarr Steps' public footpath for 100 yards to a track fork. Although 'Tarr Steps' is signed right, the track is deeply rutted, making for uncomfortable walking; our choice, though slightly longer, is to continue on the unmarked left hand fork.

Climbing to the crest of **Mounsey Hill** with views to our left, the route runs beside a hedge, swinging sharp right at a corner, parallel to another hedge, before bearing left through a gate (Wp.15 159M).

Still on open heath, we start our descent across a slope, gradually at first and then more steeply; in front are striking views of the winding **Barle Valley** and to our right, moorland and the skyline of **Winsford Hill**.

Dropping through light woodland to a path junction we bear right through a gate, picking our way down a sunken bridleway to the river. Turning right across a footbridge (Wp.16 178M) we return to the car park up the lane and scenic path (186M).

A welcome distraction might well be a cream tea with scones the size of small cottage loaves at **Tarr Farm Inn**.

Tarr Steps Clapper Bridge

Once considered to date from prehistoric times, it is more probably of late medieval origin, constructed to enable foot passengers and packhorses to cross the river **Barle**. The slabs, some weighing 5 tons, simply lie on top of supporting boulders, making this the longest *clapper bridge* on Exmoor.

Two possible derivations of the word clapper are from the Latin 'claperius' meaning 'pile of stones' and the Anglo-Saxon 'cleaca' meaning 'bridging the stepping stones'. The name 'Tarr' might derive from the Celtic 'tochar' meaning causeway.

9 PORLOCK, PITTCOMBE HEAD & HAWK COMBE

Porlock is the largest of the villages lying at the foot of steep hills surrounding **Porlock Vale**; popular as a tourist destination, it is an excellent base for hikers, offering a well stocked Information Centre plus a variety of shops, hostelries and eating places. Our varied route starts with a level stroll through woods to the interesting harbour of **Porlock Weir**, followed by a long ascent of **Worthy Combe** and a further traipse up to **Pittcombe Head**. Our reward is comfortable hilltop walking with fine coastal views across the vale; the inland return provides moorland vistas as far as **Dunkery Beacon** before dropping into **Hawk Combe** and ambling beside a stream through woods to **Porlock**.

Although GPS reception is intermittent in woods before **Porlock Weir** and poor along **Hawk Combe**, the paths and tracks are clear in both sections.

4	3¼ H	9.2 miles/14.8km		450m / 450m	↻	4*

*Porlock, Porlock Weir

Shorter Linear Route
Take the N° 300 bus to **Pittcombe Head** and join walk at Wp.10 (4.6 miles/7.4km, ascents 10 metres, descents 400 metres).

Access by bus: First bus N°38 from **Minehead** and Quantock Motor Services N°300 coast bus from **Minehead**, **Combe Martin** and **Lynton/Lynmouth**.

Access by car: **Porlock** is on the A39, 6 miles from **Minehead** and 12 miles from **Lynmouth**. Follow signs to the central car park (SS 885468).

From the top of the central car park (Wp.1 0M), we set off along the walkway between **Miles Tea and Coffee Merchants** and the Methodist church, turning right along the **High Street**, before bearing left at a road fork past the **Ship Inn** and right by the village hall onto the **Scenic Toll Road** (Wp.2 3M). Turning right onto an acorn-marked 'Porlock Weir' coast path (Wp.3 6M) we settle into an easy rhythm, striding along a level wooded path with glimpses of the wetlands bordering **Porlock Bay**.

Looking across to Hurlstone Point

Swinging round a stream and then dropping past a path junction, we go straight on up either of two paths to a wooden barrier (Wp.4 21M). Continuing ahead on the 'Footpath only to Porlock Weir' above the houses of **West Porlock**, we join the 'Porlock Weir Bridleway'. Bearing right across a footbridge with metal handrails past the village hall and over a tarmac track (Wp.5 29M), we go ahead down a short path turning left beside a metal seat onto a lane. Forking left at a **Porlock Weir** road sign along the **Toll Road**, there are views back across the bay to **Hurlstone Point**. Passing the white painted corrugated iron church and a row of cottages we go right down a lane to **Porlock Weir**, once an active harbour importing Welsh coal and limestone and exporting timber and salted herrings. Now a picturesque spot with a row of exposed cottages beside the quay, it's an interesting place for a picnic or refreshment in **The Ship Inn**.

Our route continues opposite the car park entrance beside **The Ship Inn** (Wp.6 38M) on a 'Culbone' coast path climbing through a gate then along field edges.

After a kissing gate and another gate we walk beside a left hand fence, turning right onto a lane for 100 yards, and left opposite **Worthy Manor** on a blue tipped 'Worthycombe Bridleway' (Wp.7 47M). Now we begin a long ascent up the valley between mature trees, keeping left after a house on a narrower path, following the course of the right hand stream and **Toll Road**. Although it may not always feel like it, this way is less of a struggle than tackling the 1:4 gradient up **Porlock Hill**!

Our steady ascent takes time, but it's a pleasant climb through the trees above the stream; the gradient moderates before our path reaches a T-junction where we turn right, following a red-tipped 'Culbone' sign (Wp.8 74M) along a track and over a stone bridge to a lane. After turning left for four minutes the **Toll Road** bends right; continuing straight on up the 'No through road to Pitt Farm', we go through a gate on the right of a garage to a path junction behind the buildings (Wp.9 85M).

The listed AA Box 137

Here, bearing left for 'Pittcombe Head' our track swings right uphill. Ignoring tracks off to left and right, we trudge up a steep forest track beside densely packed conifers; the end is thankfully near when we see a gate ahead and hear vehicles clunking over a cattle grid on the hilltop. Just before the road on our right is a picnic site with welcoming benches to rest and recuperate whilst enjoying views over **Porlock Bay**.

Beside the A39 (Wp.10 108M) is one of Britain's smallest listed buildings, the immaculately kept AA Box 137, a much used facility when cars spluttered their way up **Porlock Hill**, and boiled over at the top! Turning left across the **Toll Road** junction, we take a grass path heading along open hillside between the two roads; initially running close to the main road before swinging gradually left downhill. Springy turf brings welcome relief to aching calf muscles as we enjoy views across the **Bristol Channel** and down steep slopes to **Pitt Farm**; it doesn't look that far away now - as the crow flies!

Fine views over the Vale to Bossington Hill

As our path sweeps right **Porlock Vale** comes into sight with a backdrop of **Bossington Hill** and **Selworthy Beacon**; at a path T-junction (Wp.11 126M) we turn right through a car park and cross the road at **Whitstone Post**.

... our unmarked route veers sharp left ...

A 'Porlock' signpost immediately ahead (Wp.12 129M) points us diagonally left through gorse and trees. The path is indistinct for the first 50 yards until we reach a narrow path and bear left along the top of **Shillett Combe**. Enjoying a broad vista towards **Dunkery Beacon** we gently descend to a gate, then more steeply through oak trees to a path T-junction (Wp.13 145M). Turning right down a track to a lay-by cut out of the slope, our unmarked route veers sharp left onto a path dropping along the wooded hillside to a T-junction (Wp.14 152M) where we swing right on a broader track to the river.

Turning left, we wend our way along **Hawk Combe** beside a fern-lined burbling stream. The well-used track crosses two footbridges, then becomes a rough tarmac lane beyond a black and white hunting lodge. Strolling beside several interesting houses we emerge into a broadening valley floor where our lane passes the old mill and water wheel before heading along **Parsons Street** to the unusual oak shingle covered steeple of **St. Dubricius Church**, named after a Celtic saint (Wp.15 190M). Going left along the **High Street** to the post office we turn right back to the car park (Wp.16 193M).

For centuries the pursuits of hunting, shooting, fishing and riding have been part of **Exford**'s attractions; nowadays adventurous walking is certainly included. Quiet solitude is the key ingredient of this route for all seasons, as we explore countryside south of the village, a mixture of moorland, peaceful wooded slopes and lush meadows along the **Exe Valley**.

Climbing a bridleway onto Access Land at **Room Hill**, we have fine all-round views before dropping into **Curr Cleave** and returning through fields on an easy track; welcoming hostelries are located next to the large village green and beside the picturesque river bridge.

2/3 — 2¼ H — 6.1 miles/9.8km — 250m / 250m — 3*

*at **Exford**

Access by bus: First bus N°398 limited service from **Tiverton** and **Dulverton**

Access by car: **Exford** is on the B3224, 5 miles west of **Wheddon Cross**. From **Dulverton** (10 miles) and **Lynton** (15 miles) take the B3223. The car park is in the village (SS 854384).

> **Extended walk**
> Combine this route with Walk 7 for a figure of eight walk along the **Exe** valley and surrounding hills. Just before Wp.9 turn right to join Walk 7 at Wp.7. Return from **Winsford** along the outward section of Walk 7 and rejoin this walk (11.3 miles/18.2km ascents & descents 470 metres).

Heading away from the village (SE) through the car park (Wp.1 0M) and past the **National Park Field Services Centre** takes us straight out into the countryside, strolling through riverside meadows and kissing gates to a concrete bridge where we turn right across the **Exe** (Wp.2 6M).

Turning left between houses at a blue painted 'Room Hill' sign, we walk along a tarmac lane past **Court Farm** and where the lane bears right, go straight on through a gate (Wp.3 9M) up a rough sunken track.

Climbing steadily around a field edge our path narrows as we reach the top of a rise; the way ahead on an 'alternative route for walkers' is considerably easier underfoot than the adjacent churned up bridleway.

We rejoin the bridleway for a short stiff climb beside **Court Copse** which brings us to a gate and an easier gradient, straight across rough pasture with views back to **Exford** and over open moors.

Magnificent beech trees

After going though a gate (Wp.4 28M) we turn immediately right on a 'Bridleway' climbing beside a hedge-bank through two fields onto moorland; to our left, magnificent rows of mature beech trees form substantial boundaries.

Still keeping parallel to the hedge-bank taking either of the two tracks ahead, we arrive at a large tree (Wp.5 38M) and fork left; our path dips slightly then curves up (S) around the top of a small *combe*.

Enjoying views into Curr Cleave

Looking out for a small finger post tucked into gorse bushes on our left, we fork left for 'Winsford' (Wp.6 44M) striding out over **Room Hill** and bearing gently left (ESE) across the common. The views ahead are of **Winsford Hill**; on our left, the bracken-covered slopes of **Curr Cleave** fall steeply down to the **Exe**, while **Dunkery Beacon** stands out on the horizon.

Down the Exe Valley to Bye Common

We continue straight on along a grass path, then turn left 100 yards before a hedge and gate (Wp.7 51M), heading downhill for a minute before bearing right on a well-defined earth and stone path; dropping down the side of a tree filled *combe*, lovely distant views of **Bye Common** are replaced by the sinuous **Exe Valley**.

Turning right along the river bank for 100 yards and going through a metal gate on our right (Wp.8 62M), we bear left across a field to a yellow stake where a short section of track leads us through a gate; at the far end of a narrow field our path squeezes through a bank, becoming narrower as we stroll through light woodland beside the **Exe**.

Stepping onto a dirt track (turn right for the extended walk) across a bridge, then left on a 'Permitted Exford Path' (Wp.9 74M), we amble through riverside fields along a quiet wooded valley. After bearing right at a 'Footpath' sign (Wp.10 80M), we climb past a tumbled down bank to a gate (Wp.11 83M). Going left on a bridleway onto Access Land, we come to a junction where we fork right along a hillside track; another option is to take the left track to a pleasant riverside picnic spot, then meander through pastures before rejoining the higher path.

Our wide bridleway runs along the steep side of **Curr Cleave** above the tree-lined river; stretching our legs on an easy track through unspoilt countryside, the valley gradually opens out as we enter fields and follow a track down to **Lyncombe Farm**, noticing a moss-covered packhorse bridge through a gate on our left.

After the farm gate we go immediately left over a stile into a field (Wp.12 109M); our yellow-marked path starts off beside a right hand hedge then curves left through a marshy bit of ground to the river edge, crossing three more stiles in quick succession. Going through a gate and walking slightly uphill behind gorse bushes, we bear diagonally left along a field slope to a gate and stream (Wp.13 119M) then continue beside a right hand hedge to a pedestrian gate. Turning left, our path swings right across a field and through a gate; heading down a left hand track to a concrete bridge we turn right along the river bank to **Exford** (Wp.14 133M).

11 ROMANCING WITH LORNA DOONE - ROBBER'S BRIDGE, OARE & DOONE VALLEY

There can be few historical novels that have become so woven into the fabric of real life that **Doone Country** now appears on maps and a real church window is labelled as 'the actual window' through which the villain shoots the heroine on her fictional wedding day! Whether or not we are familiar with the story, our route takes us to three superb locations said to have been part of the inspiration for R D Blackmore's romantic 17th century adventure; even without reading the book to check if the heroine survives, this is a thoroughly enjoyable walk.

Our route from **Robber's Bridge** is along a deep wooded valley to the interesting **Oare Church**, then onto **Cloud Farm** and through the touristy bit of **Badgworthy Water**'s gorgeous woods. Heading further south up the less visited but equally beautiful river valley, we return across open country with moors as far as the eye can see, before our descent to **Weir Water**.

| 3 | 3 H | 8¾ miles/14km | 320m 320m | | 2 |

Public transport: Minehead-Lynmouth Blue Bus Nº34 to **Oare Church** Wednesday only.

Access by car: reach **Robber's Bridge** car park (SS 820464) from A39 near **County Gate**, signed 'Malmsmead and Oare', turning left at **Oare Church**.

Stroll: Weir Water Easy Access Route
A fifty minute, 1¾ mile/2.8km circular amble has been created along a moorland stretch of **Weir Water**. Turning left out of **Robber's Bridge** car park along the lane for 200 yards we join the river bank on our right to the information board. This level route with lovely valley views runs beside the stream, crossing a footbridge to return along the opposite bank.

Starting from the car park (Wp.1 0M) we turn right across **Robber's Bridge** strolling (W) along the lane beside **Weir Water** towards **Oare**.

Stretching our legs, we enjoy easy level walking all the way to **Oare Church** along a deep valley with steep slopes covered in woods and pastures (Wp.2 29M). In the novel, this church was the location for Lorna and John's interrupted wedding; today, visitors cross the solid oak threshold of this simple white washed building to identify the window from where … 'the sound of a shot rang through the church'.

Oare Church

Leaving the lane immediately before **Oare Church** via a field gate on our left signed 'Bridleway South Common, Larkbarrow', we climb steeply beside a

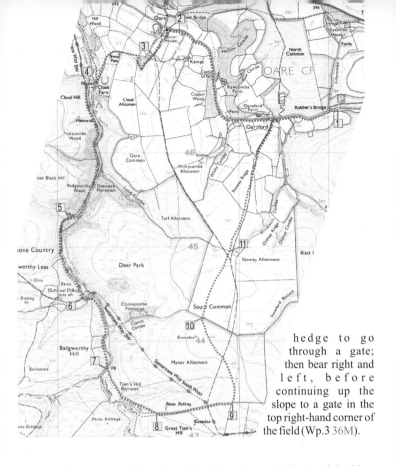

hedge to go through a gate; then bear right and left, before continuing up the slope to a gate in the top right-hand corner of the field (Wp.3 36M).

Going straight on we follow the 'Cloud Farm, Doone Valley' path beside a small *combe* to swing right at the top then right again at the gate. After 25 yards, before reaching the next gate, we turn left beside the right hand stone wall; there are views of the hills between **Lynton** and **Porlock** and the moorland lies ahead. Beyond the gate at the brow of the hill, we walk down the grassy path into the **Doone Valley**, then beneath the stilts of a tall farm building, going through a right hand gate past a red telephone box to **Cloud Farm Tea Room** (Wp.4 50M).

Badgworthy Water

Crunching down the gravel path beside the car park we follow the 'Doone Valley' signs, crossing a footbridge over **Badgworthy Water** (pronounced Badgery) and turning left at the blue bridleway sign along the valley. For the next mile or so we are in real tourist country and it is easy to see why this is such a popular location; a pretty river surrounded by oak clad hills, rocky outcrops and moor. This atmospheric setting is reenforced by a Memorial Stone inscribed "to the memory of Richard Doddridge Blackmore whose novel Lorna Doone extols to all the world the joys of Exmoor". Keeping to the main dirt track we stroll along the valley floor, the moorland river on our left constantly changes; one moment jam packed with stones and rushing water, the next a tranquil flow.

Passing through a gate we arrive at a footbridge crossing the **Lankcombe** stream (Wp.5 72M); on our right the smooth moss covered boulders could well be the fictional rockslide where our young hero and heroine first meet. Now our path becomes narrower as it climbs above the river, giving us the opportunity to enjoy this beautiful valley and contrasting vegetation; in early summer invasive purple rhododendrons claw their way up the left hand slope to the skyline. Although impressive, they are not an indigenous species; the ancient deciduous oak woodland on our side of the river is the natural landscape.

As the tourists thin out we pass a 'Larkbarrow and Brendon Common' waymark and continue walking for 5 minutes to arrive at a 'Brendon Common' sign (Wp.6 85M); before us in **Hoccombe Combe** grass mounds cover the ruins of a medieval village, the possible hideout of the legendary Carver Doone and his outlaws. Forking left down a grass path, we go ahead through a gate in the tree lined wall, walking the plank across a stream, before keeping left along the river valley.

The scenery around us now changes to wilder rock strewn slopes and moorland as we follow the path to a gate in the stone wall and over a river footbridge (Wp.7 97M), turning right up a track between the hummocks of **Tom's Hill Barrows**. Our path soon descends, then swings left uphill in front of a stone wall as we steadily climb to go through a gate (Wp.8 110M); ignoring the direction sign, we turn left (E) alongside the stone and earth bank to a bridleway gate (Wp.9 122M).

The signpost at Wp.10

As we turn left for 'Oareford', we're totally surrounded by a moorland expanse of grass, *combes* and gently rolling hills; our gradually ascending route along a less distinct path starts off north, then curves gently left (NNW). Weaving over a short section of boggy ground we reach a gate in a fence (Wp.10 135M) and following the same direction signs, we head on (NNE), gently climbing to the brow of **South Common**, a large pasture with terrific 360 degree views.

Cresting the hill we have a grand view ahead of the hills beyond the **Oare Valley** and glimpses of the sea; aiming for a dip ahead in the far hills we pass a marker post standing in the field to reach a gate (Wp.11 145M). Our route continues towards 'Oareford' as we head just right of the fingerpost sign, following a slight mound marking the downhill route of an old grass covered track. Passing through another gate, the track becomes more defined as we continue steadily down in the same direction, before a final steep descent to the lane where we turn right to **Robber's Bridge** (174M).

12 COMBE MARTIN, HOLDSTONE HILL AND THE HANGMANS

This cracking route provides exhilarating walking with a stunning combination of coast and inland vistas from start to finish. The medieval village of **Combe Martin** at the north-west edge of the National Park claims to have the longest main street in England, nearly two miles in length; fortunately we need cover only a short part of it, near the sea front.

Climbing ancient tracks to a ridge, we stroll along quiet country lanes and field paths to a high point at **Holdstone Hill**; after joining the **South West Coast Path** we have a sharp drop into **Sherrycombe**, then a climb to the summit of **Great Hangman**, the South West's highest cliff. Our cliff top return goes through an area designated as **Heritage Coast** because of its natural unspoilt beauty.

| 4 | 3H * | 8.3 miles/13.4km | 630m / 630m | ↻ | 3* |

*at Combe Martin

Access by bus: First bus N°30 from **Barnstaple** and **Ilfracombe**, Quantock Motor Services N°300 from **Taunton**, **Minehead** and **Ilfracombe**.

Access by car: **Combe Martin** on the A399 is 5 miles from both **Ilfracombe** and **Blackmoor Gate**; the main car park (SS 578473) is next to the beach.

Shorter walk
Turn left at Wp.6 for **Great Hangman**, taking a track through fields and rejoining the route at Wp.14 (4¾ miles/7.6km, ascents & descents 350 metres).

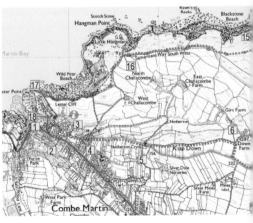

From the large seafront car park (Wp.1 0M) and turning left beside the National Park Information Centre in **Cross Street**, we continue along the main street.

Opposite a 'King Street' sign, we turn left on a 'Public Footpath' into a narrow tarmac alley (Wp.2 3M).

After passing the school and **Old Forge** house (Wp.3 5M) we bear right up a 'Public Footpath for Great Hangman and Little Hangman', starting our climb and going across a road onto a 'Rocky Lane to Knapdown' (Wp.4 7M). This centuries old sunken track lives up to its name and it's easy to conjure up images of stealthy smugglers in the dead of night.

Joining a road, we trudge on uphill to a seat with a commemorative plaque delightfully inscribed 'Morning Coffee', pausing to look down over **Combe Martin Bay**. A few paces beyond, going left on a public footpath signed 'Great Hangman Knapdown Lane' (Wp.5 20M) we steadily climb the length of a ridge with views opening up to **Watermouth Bay** and **Little Hangman**.

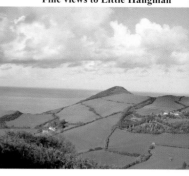

To the Silver Mines

As the gradient eases, the vista extends beyond a sweeping valley across the **Bristol Channel** as far as the **Gower Peninsula**, while ahead a moorland fringe hides the top of **Great Hangman**.

At **Knap Down Lane Head** (Wp.6 36M) the shorter route goes left for 'Great Hangman', while our route turns right to follow a track aptly named 'Silver Mines'. Precious metals were extracted in this area for hundreds of years until mining ended over a century ago.

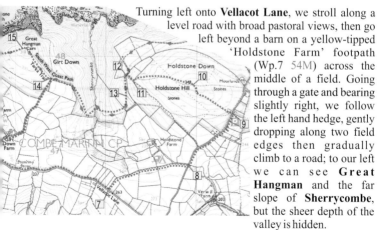

Turning left onto **Vellacot Lane**, we stroll along a level road with broad pastoral views, then go left beyond a barn on a yellow-tipped 'Holdstone Farm' footpath (Wp.7 54M) across the middle of a field. Going through a gate and bearing slightly right, we follow the left hand hedge, gently dropping along two field edges then gradually climb to a road; to our left we can see **Great Hangman** and the far slope of **Sherrycombe**, but the sheer depth of the valley is hidden.

Using stone steps we climb over a bank (Wp.8 68M) and turn left up a road then left again beneath a car park height restrictor (Wp.9 78M) and straight on up a grass path onto **Holdstone Down**. Behind us an undulating green patchwork quilt (see picture over page) stretches across **Parracombe** to the ridge between **Shilstone Hill** and **Brendon Two Gates**; equally splendid are the grand coastal views including the silhouette of **Lundy Island**.

Keeping left by a cairn marking the summit of **Holdstone Hill** (Wp.10 86M 349 metres) we descend a path between heather and gorse and after crossing a tumbledown wall, turn right at a path crossroads (Wp.11 95M).

Going down a rough track to a T-junction, we turn left on the 'Coast Path' (Wp.12 97M), then bear right at a 'Combe Martin' sign (Wp.13 100M) heading towards the bulk of **Great Hangman.** As the gradient steepens, the depth of **Sherrycombe** suddenly becomes apparent; plunging to the valley floor, we negotiate a squeeze stile and cross a footbridge. Toiling across steep contours on a narrow earth path, we swing right just before a stone wall and after heading seawards, bear left alongside a field boundary to **Blackstone Point Cross** (Wp.14 125M). The timing for this section is quite arbitrary, we timed this on a crisp November day but have taken a lot longer in July!

... dropping steadily along cliff tops ...

Going straight on up a heather clad slope to a cairn on top of **Great Hangman** (Wp.15 132M 318 metres) our route is displayed around us complete with a moorland background and an unspoilt **Heritage Coast**. Now we can put the book away, striding out on a terrific section of coast path and dropping steadily along cliff tops towards glorious views.

At a 'Little Hangman' sign (Wp.16 151M) it's worth clambering to the summit bench for views of **Watermouth Bay**. Then it's back down onto the coast path, along cliff and field edges, before a short climb between hedgerows to a shelter; just beyond, bearing right at a path fork (Wp.17 173M) we emerge onto a grass sward above **Combe Martin Bay** and swing left to the car park (Wp.18 179M).

13 STARK CONTRASTS! HEDDON VALLEY AND HOLDSTONE HILL

The beautiful secluded **Heddon Valley** is a marvellous place to start this exhilarating, starkly contrasting walk of dramatic cliffs and tranquil wooded valleys cutting down to the sea. These massive cliffs, some of southern England's highest, give wonderful coastal views as well as a far-reaching inland panorama; south for 30 miles to Dartmoor's distinctive northern profile, east across a pastoral patchwork quilt to Exmoor's open moorland.

From **Hunter's Inn** we have an easy stroll along the valley to the coast at **Heddon's Mouth** before tackling the steep slog past **Peter Rock** to the cliff edge. Then we can quicken our stride along the high coast path to **Holdstone Down** where we turn inland for a steady climb of **Holdstone Hill**. Our final descent encompasses open heath with superb far-reaching views, the sylvan sheltered oasis of the level **Ladies' Mile Path** and a tree-lined river.

4	3½ H	9.8 miles/15½km	↗ 500m ↘ 500m	⚠ *	↻	🍴 2 🍽

* along a short part of the cliff path near **Peter Rock**

Access by car: from A39 between **Parracombe** and **Lynton** signposted 'Heddon's Mouth and Hunter's Inn' (SS655482). Park on the road near **Hunter's Inn** or in the National Trust car park beside the shop and toilets.

Stroll
From **Hunter's Inn** follow the route to **Heddon's Mouth** and then back along the other side of the river (2 miles/3.2km).

Shorter route
From Wp.9, turn left up the track to reach the road and turn right, rejoining the main walk at Wp.13 (2¾ hours, 8 miles/12.8km).

From the National Trust shop (Wp.1 0M) we head towards **Hunter's Inn** and bear right up the road for 25 yards before walking straight ahead onto a broad woodland track signed 'Heddon's Mouth 1'. Passing the five-barred gate we turn left on the signed bridleway to stroll through mature woodland beside the river. When the well-used path forks, we keep left to stay beside the river to reach a stone bridge (Wp.2 10M); if you don't want to visit **Heddon's Mouth**, cross the bridge to join the path on the other side of the river at Wp.4.

The Heddon Valley (near Wp.3)

Beyond the bridge with the river on our left, our path abruptly emerges from the steep wooded slopes into a surprising barren landscape of scree-covered hillsides. The whole valley has a wild feel about it as if we have been hurled back to the end of the Ice Age. High up to our left, the imposing height of **Peter Rock** awaits and any Ice Age thoughts melt away as we anticipate the hot climb to come! Crossing the rushing river on a wooden footbridge we turn right to reach the shingle beach at **Heddon's Mouth** (Wp.3 20M). Although not much of a recreational beach today, in the 18th and 19th centuries, coasters from South Wales landed coal and limestone here, returning with pit props cut from the Exmoor forests for the Welsh mines. The circular coal fired lime kiln built into the bank produced lime to improve the acid soil.

Retracing our steps to the footbridge, we go straight ahead with the river on our left for half a mile, passing the shortcut path on our left (Wp.4 29M), to the next signpost 'Coast path to Combe Martin' (Wp.5 32M). Turning right and leaving the tree line below, we start our long climb, the gradient increasing as our path zigzags up between heather and scree; happily, there are benches from where we can admire the dramatic views. Our path finally levels out for us to revel in a birds-eye view of the valley from river mouth to **Hunter's Inn**. Passing below **Peter Rock** (Wp.6 53M) we turn left along the coast path, being careful along this exposed narrow section; especially if it is wet underfoot or in windy conditions. Our uphill route twists and turns as we pick our way round rocky outcrops with a steep drop to the sea on our right.

Suddenly the views open up, revealing the smooth contours of **Trentishoe Down** and **Holdstone Hill** , plus distant views of **Widmouth Head, Lundy Island** and across the **Bristol Channel** to South Wales. Completing our ascent of **East Cleave** to a path junction (Wp.7 66M) we turn right along the cliff top, rewarded with superb open-cliff walking to **Holdstone Down**, time to enjoy the stunning views with a well-earned breather and picnic. These are *hog's-back cliffs* where the land angles downwards before wave power erosion causes them to drop vertically into the sea. On our left lies **Trentishoe Down**, frequented by intrepid hang gliders, however, with our feet firmly on the springy turf we stride out beside the earth banked field boundaries to follow a 'Coast path through gate, turn right' sign before dropping down a short flight of steps to see our path crossing the field ahead.

Looking back to Heddon's Mouth

Leaving the cliff edge through a gate (Wp.8 89M), our route cuts diagonally right into a dip, bearing left up the field through a gate onto the heath. The clear stony track climbs gently, levelling out after 10 minutes to bear right at a coast path sign for 'Combe Martin'. Soon reaching another junction (Wp.9 107M), we go right along a broad grass track.

From Wp.9 the shorter route turns left up to the road and then right to a signpost marked 'Trentishoe Mill' at Wp.13. Our track, originally constructed as a coast road to move cargo from remote landing points, passes through a landscape of heather and bracken. We gently descend **Holdstone Down**, enjoying views ahead of the steep slopes of **Sherrycombe** falling to the sea in front of the looming mass of **Great Hangman**. Turning sharply inland, our route rises and bends right; after 100 yards at a 'County Road' sign on our left we leave the coast path (Wp.10 127M) to climb the stony track for 100 yards to a path intersection (Wp.11 129M) and turn left. In 20 yards we zigzag right and left through a gap in the broken down stone wall, ascending the narrow path (E) through gorse and onto the open heath of **Holdstone Hill**. The cairn and trig point (349m Wp.12 141M) mark our walk's summit, the spectacular 360° views just reward for our efforts - time to marvel at the coastal views and gaze inland towards the heart of Exmoor. On a clear day there are long distant views to Dartmoor's northern slopes.

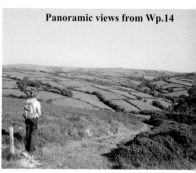

Panoramic views from Wp.14

Now it's all down hill. Turning our backs on the splendours of the rugged coastline we head straight down the wide track (E), not the path on our right, to reach the road (Wp.13 149M). Crossing the road we follow the 'Trentishoe Mill 1½ miles' sign along a grassy permissive track drifting gently downhill towards a panorama of deep wooded valleys and patchwork fields. At a track junction (Wp.14 157M) we bear slightly left off the broad track down a path (SE), marked with a white arrow on a small wooden stake.

Passing the corner of a stone boundary wall, our path descends steeply entering mixed deciduous woodland, curving left along the side of the valley to reach a T-junction with the 'Ladies' Mile Path' (Wp.15 168M); this last section of the path surface is quite loose and can be eroded after heavy rain. Turning left for an easy stroll along the edge of the woodland it is easy to see how this sheltered spot encourages early flowering of various plants; when walking this route at the end of October purple rhododendrons were in bloom, contrasting vividly with the blanched trunks of silver birches.

We cross a path junction and continue to a road, turning right for a few steps to the **Rhyddabank** crossroads and right again signed 'Millham'. We immediately turn left (Wp.16 187M) on the **Hunter's Inn** footpath to head down through mature woodland to reach the river bank. Following the track alongside the small river on our right, we join a lane turning right to reach the welcome sight of **Hunter's Inn** (Wp.17 207M).

Big skies, wide horizons and colourful natural carpets dominate this linear trek connecting two of Exmoor's highest features, the village of **Wheddon Cross** and the cairn on top of **Dunkery Beacon**. Our route takes in **Snowdrop Valley**, one of Exmoor's harbingers of spring, when swathes of snowdrops abound. Strolling upstream beside the charming **River Avill** we climb the moor to **Dunkery** where woodland gives way to heather, especially striking in late summer when the slopes are covered in purple and magenta.

Enjoying widespread views, we head down to the village of **Wootton Courtenay** and then climb very steeply through woods to a high ridge running east to **Grabbist Hill**; a comfortable skyline walk offers tremendous coastal views before our final descent to **Dunster**. This large village has many tourist attractions including a prominent castle and a good variety of cafes and inns, or, if you are in a hurry, we recommend the takeaway cream tea from the deli. A GPS or compass should be carried in case of poor visibility.

5 | 4½ H | 12.4 miles/20km | 600m / 850m | 3*

* at **Wheddon Cross, Dunster**

Shorter route
At Wp.15 continue on lanes to **Cowbridge Cross** turning right to A396 and right to **Timberscombe** (10 miles/16km, ascents 350m, descents 600m).

Access by bus: First bus N°398 connects **Minehead-Dunster-Wheddon Cross-Dulverton** and **Tiverton**. **Dunster**'s bus stop is in the **High Street**.

Access by car: **Dunster** is 3 miles from **Minehead** on the A396; ½ mile from the junction with A39. Park in the car park by the Information Centre (SS 993439). If parking at **Wheddon Cross** use the car park on A396 next to **The Rest and Be Thankful Inn** (SS 924388)

From **Wheddon Cross** car park (Wp.1 0M) turning left past **The Rest and Be Thankful Inn** along the A396, we bear right by the war memorial then fork left along a lane through **Cutcombe**. After passing **St. John's Church** and a couple of yappy farm dogs we climb a short rise to a left hand gate, inside, a 'Footpath' sign (Wp.2 15M) points us around the right hand field edge. Curving down to the tree line and a pedestrian gate, (Wp.3 20M) our track drops to the A396 road. Crossing carefully onto a 'Footpath to Drapers Way', we bear left after 100 yards along a woodland track, gradually descending to a lane (Wp.4 35M).

We go ahead through an unmarked gate. Every February the valley floor is covered

Snowdrop Valley

with millions of snowdrops and many folk make an annual pilgrimage to enjoy a white and green-flecked floral carpet that brightens even the gloomiest winter's day. After 200 yards we bear left through a gate (Wp.5 38M) and gently climb through a field, curving left to a track crossroads (Wp.6 43M); going straight ahead through gates and rough pastures (WSW) we gradually swing right onto a blue marked 'Bridleway' by a stone bridge (Wp.7 47M). Our pretty woodland track winds along the valley side with the **River Avill** on our right; sploshing across side streams, we follow several 'Dunkery Gate Bridleway' signs.

Through a gate and continuing ahead at a signpost, we start to climb before turning left at another signpost (Wp.8 61M) heading up into rough pasture. The path gradually peters out but we continue in the same direction (W) dipping very slightly then keeping beside a right hand hedgerow. Where a line of trees in front meets the hedge we through go a blue-marked gate tucked into the right corner (Wp.9 72M). Climbing straight up a hillside for 100 yards to a track T-junction, we turn left (W) along a stony track over open moorland to a road at **Dunkery Gate** (Wp.10 86M). Turning right for 100 yards, then left up a 'Dunkery Beacon bridleway', we climb steadily through moorland heather to the summit cairn (Wp.11 103M); on a clear day there is a great panorama and our first coastal views. Turning right, we stride along a level stretch of track, which on a summer Saturday can be nearly as busy as Oxford Street, then re-cross the road onto a 'Brockwell bridleway' (Wp12 119M). Losing the crowds and heading downhill (NE) the ground soon flattens as we bear gently right at a path fork (Wp13 124M) (ENE) on a broad track.

Rounding the shoulder of a hill we face a lengthy moorland descent on a rutted track to **Wootton Courtenay**; fortunately fine valley and ridge views are a welcome distraction and the going gradually improves closer to the trees. Staying on the main path through a lightly wooded area, the soil underfoot changes from dark peaty brown to deep red as we bend right and drop to a lane. Turning left for 150 yards to a road sign at **Brockwell** (Wp14 164M), we veer right down a lane to 'Wootton Courtenay', the smooth surface a welcome relief as we bear right at a road junction through the village. After **All Saints'**

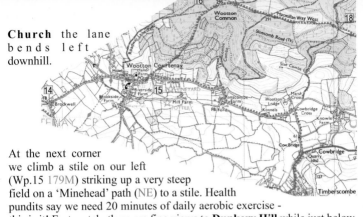

Church the lane bends left downhill.

At the next corner we climb a stile on our left (Wp.15 179M) striking up a very steep field on a 'Minehead' path (NE) to a stile. Health pundits say we need 20 minutes of daily aerobic exercise - this is it! Fortunately there are fine views to **Dunkery Hill** while just below, vines ripen on a south-facing slope. Entering trees, our steep ascent continues (NE) past a forest road junction onto a wider track for 50 yards. Looking carefully on our left for a red and yellow marker post, we go through a bank up a narrow path - in fact it's more like a narrow trench to start with. Bearing right at a T-junction we soon follow a 'Minehead' sign straight on uphill over a forest track, keeping right as the gradient finally eases onto a forest road. At the next junction (Wp.16 201M) a 'Bridleway' sign points us right along a dirt road to a blue marker; going through a left hand gap we turn right at a 'Dunster' sign (Wp.17 206M). Now high on a ridge, our exertions are rewarded with a wonderful coastal panorama including **Minehead** and the white tented pavilions of Butlin's far below. Along our trail we see **Watchet,** the **Quantock Hills** and over the **Bristol Channel** to **Wales**; **Dunster Castle** lies ahead and to its left is **Conygar Tower**, a square shaped folly. Gradually descending along the broad 'Dunster Bridleway' (E) we continue straight ahead at a second crossroads (Wp.18 220M) to a third at **Holes Corner**. Going ahead, we fork right as our path divides to continue along the ridge, enjoying splendid inland views of valleys, mixed woodlands, fields and high hills.

At a National Trust **Grabbist Hill** plaque (Wp.19 246M), choose your route off the ridge; the sensible way is to turn right diagonally down the slope to the next waypoint.

For a short detour to admire a grand view over **Dunster** village and castle, continue ahead, swinging right to a vantage point then retracing our steps to the NT plaque. However, if you decide to continue straight down (the GPS route) be prepared for an extremely steep adventurous path, grabbing at trees during a slither-and-slide descent to meet the sensible walkers at the bottom (Wp.20 260M). Going through a gate ahead onto a tarmac track beside allotments we bend right down the slope ambling past the school to a T-junction. Turning right, then immediately left into **Priory Green** beside **St George's Church** lych-gate, our lane runs past the Memorial Gardens between quaint thatched houses to join the main street (Wp.21 269M) where we turn left for the car park (271M).

15 ROADWATER, NETTLECOMBE & MONKSILVER CIRCULAR

The parishes of **Monksilver, Nettlecombe** and **Old Cleeve** lie just inside the eastern boundary of **Exmoor National Park**; a peaceful landscape of pastures, woods, rolling hills and secluded valleys. Along our way there are wonderful far reaching views to the **Quantocks** and back across the **Brendon Hills** and Exmoor.

Our hilly route from the village of **Roadwater** heads east through lanes and fields on yellow-marked footpaths, including several stiles, to **Nettlecombe Court**; an impressive country house with its own church in a mature parkland setting. An easier section follows along a small river valley to the pretty village of **Monksilver** and a 14th century church. Our return on part of the **Coleridge Way** uses gated bridleways for a steady climb over **Bird's Hill** to **Chidgley,** finishing with a comfortable stroll along a sheltered valley above the line of an old railway.

Access by bus: Webberbus N°564, limited service from **Minehead**, Wednesday and Friday.

Access by car: Roadwater is 7 miles from **Minehead** and 20 miles from Taunton. At **Washford** on the A39, turn south on **Abbey Road**. After ½ mile bear right on a lane for 1½ miles. Park in the village on the wider section of road or in the lay-by beyond **The Valiant Soldier Inn**.

Shorter Walk

From Wp.7, turn right past **Nettlecombe Court**, taking right hand yellow footpath for B3190 over field and along a grass path up valley and through wood to road, turning left for 650 yards to **Chidgley Hill Farm** house. Turn right through gate following the permitted 'Roadwater' sign, to go behind the large barn and through gate along blue marked 'Roadwater valley' track, to Wp.14 (5.9 miles/9½km, ascents & descents 325 metres).

Midway (ST031382) between **Roadwater** Post Office and the **Valiant Soldier Inn** is a sign 'Road narrows to 9 foot width' (Wp.1 0M) ; going along this lane beside Rose Villa and Lyndale we climb steeply out of the village to a stile (Wp.2 6M) and turn left on a 'Chidgley via Kingsdown' path. Leaving the woodland over a stile, going left then left again over a second stile, we bear right up the right hand field boundary.

Views back to Wp.3

Slogging uphill across a double stile, the gradient steepens until we reach the corner of a copse; here we head diagonally right over a hilltop to a gateway and lane (Wp.3 21M). Crossing over, we ascend a wide track to go through a

gap in a hedge (Wp.4 24M); zigzagging immediately right and left, we climb beside a left-hand hedge to the summit. After these exertions, this is a good spot to rest and take in the grand picture enjoying the full impact of views back to **North Hill**, **Lype Hill**, and over to **Wales**.

Walking beside the left hand hedge to a stile (Wp.5 29M) we go straight on for 'Nettlecombe'; now with hedge rows on our right, we

Nettlecombe Court and St Mary's Church
There's been a Manor House here since at least 1160, passed down through generations of the related families of Ralegh, Whalesborough, Trevelyan and Wolseley. The house today dates from 1600, set in an 18th century parkland of fields and mature trees. Leased by the Field Studies Council, this Site of Special Scientific Interest is used as an education centre. The undisturbed environment supports a wide variety of flora and fauna, notably lichen and over 50 varieties of wood boring beetles thriving on dead timber which is left to rot in situ. The 12th century parish church has many interesting features including tomb recesses containing ancestral effigies of the Ralegh family.

stretch our legs on a gradual descent (ESE) through pastures and over stiles onto a track leading to a lane. Glorious views open up of the **Quantocks** and **North Somerset**; the two islands in the middle of the **Bristol Channel** are **Steep Holm** and **Flat Holm**. Crossing a stile (Wp.6 38M) into mature parkland above **Nettlecombe Court,** we bear left to drop between red labelled veteran oaks to cross a stile by a metal gate in the corner of a left hand field. Strolling down the parkland edge passing several huge sweet chestnuts, we cross another stile to a path junction; turning right on a short section of stony track onto a tarmac lane, we descend beside the church to a junction with **Nettlecombe Court** drive (Wp.7 49M). Information boards about the house and estate are on our right.

Turning left along the drive beside a small arboretum, we bear left over a stile down a grass 'public bridleway' to a lane; a few yards further on, crossing a right hand stile to 'Monksilver' (Wp.8 60M) we climb straight ahead over a mound keeping the trees on our left. Descending to cross two stiles in quick succession and keeping slightly left, we amble beside a meandering stream along a meadow; negotiating patches of sticky red clay and scrubland, we go left through a pedestrian gate (Wp.9 71M) over a rivulet and up a hillock to a kissing-gate. Our enclosed woodland track on a low wooded escarpment becomes a permitted path beside a field edge, before turning left down a flight of steps and right into **Monksilver**. Continuing through **Pond Orchard** towards the church, we fork left at a red telephone box on a path beside the churchyard, turning left by the gate for refreshments at **The Notley Arms** (Wp.10 80M).

Suitably fortified, our route continues along part of the **Coleridge Way** (0M) on a churchyard path to the left of **All Saints Church**, turning right onto a lane beside **The Old School House** and its tiny bell tower. After turning left beside **The Old Rectory** on a 'Roadwater' path, we start our lengthy climb, trudging steadily up **Bird's Hill** through a kissing-gate to the tree line, then right up a blue marked bridleway (Wp.11 10M). Our sunken lane wriggles its way onwards and upwards between fern and bracken covered banks; eventually, as the gradient lessens, it becomes a pleasant woodland path and in autumn we kick our way through a carpet of fallen leaves to **Colton Cross**.

Going straight ahead up the lane a sign indicates a short detour to a viewpoint across the **Bristol Channel**; back in the lane we continue to a gate, turning right onto 'Chidgley bridleway' (Wp.12 41M). Climbing ahead to a woodland corner and through a gate into the wood, we go straight across a path junction, gradually descending an earth track. From this elevated position there are big valley views and the scale of the parkland and stands of trees surrounding **Nettlecombe Court** can be fully appreciated. Keeping right for 'Roadwater', our track reaches the B3190; taking care, we turn right on this busy road, crossing to the left hand verge before a sharp bend. Passing a minor road we take the next track on our left (Wp.13 56M) beside **Chidgley Hill Farm** gate, going along a grass track and through a metal gate to a track junction (Wp.14 60M).

Turning left through a wooden gate, we bear right beneath a long row of trees and keeping them on our right, commence our well marked gradual descent to **Roadwater**. Lengthening our stride, we head along the side of a secluded open valley before entering **Pit Wood** then out along the field edges; the lane below follows the line of an old mineral railway that carried iron ore from the **Brendon Hills** to **Watchet** until 1910.

Going through a small wood, we swing across a clearing and stream into **Erridge Wood**; continuing straight ahead, our path then bears right on a level pine needle track leading to a field and lane (Wp.15 96M). Turning left over **Roadwater**'s original level-crossing, there are two other railway relics on our right, old track support girders and the station platform; passing **The Old Bakery**, we return to our start point (98M).

16 LYNMOUTH, WATERSMEET AND COUNTISBURY

Lynmouth Harbour & Rhenish Tower

The attractive seaside village of **Lynmouth** with its small harbour is a bustling tourist centre for much of the year, offering a variety of shops, hotels and eating places. In a landscape dominated by densely wooded ravines and towering sea cliffs, the combined forces of **East** and **West Lyn** rivers flow into the **Bristol Channel**.

Starting from the **Rhenish Tower**, we stroll on a well used path up the river valley to the pretty sylvan setting of **Watersmeet House**; after a stiff climb through secluded oak woods to **South Hill Common** we are rewarded by splendid inland vistas. Our return from **Countisbury Church** takes in one of the most spectacular sections of the coast path, offering superb views of **Lynton**, **Lynmouth** and **Foreland Point**. (GPS reception is poor between Wp.2 & 3)

3 | 2 H | 5¾ miles/9¼km | 320m / 320m | 4

Access by bus: from **Barnstaple** N°s309 and 310 From **Minehead** and **Ilfracombe** N°300.

Access by car: Lynmouth (SS 723494) is on the A39, 11 miles from both **Blackmoor Gate** and **Porlock**. Car parking in the village.

Extension 1
Take the **Cliff Railway** to **Lynton** and turn right to the Town Hall to join Walk 17. (10¼ miles /16.5km, ascents & descents 550 metres)

Extension 2
From **Countisbury Churchyard** Wp.6, turn right to join Walk 18 at Wp.19. Continue to **Barna Barrow** then follow Walk 18, rejoining Walk 16 at **Countisbury Church**. (13 miles/ 21km, ascents & descents 720 metres)

East Lyn Valley

From the **Rhenish Tower** (Wp.1 0M), we stroll beside the harbour wall, going left over the white footbridge then right up a tarmac path through the park to cross the busy A39 into **Tors Road** (Wp.2 4M). At the crest our lane bears right, back down to the riverbank where we head upstream past a string of Victorian hotels, guest houses and holiday lets. The boulder-strewn **East Lyn** tumbles towards us through a narrowing V-shaped valley between densely wooded slopes; this

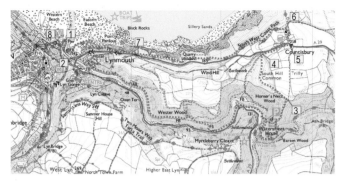

area was dubbed "Little Switzerland" by the Romantic poets Shelley, Coleridge and Wordsworth. Strolling beside a wall above the river we soon pass the last of the houses to join a riverside path; following signs to 'Watersmeet' and ignoring a footbridge, we continue straight on with the river on our right. Our stony way climbs past a 'path closed due to landslip' sign (at the time of research) before gradually descending to a junction (26M).

The site of Lynrock Mineral Factory

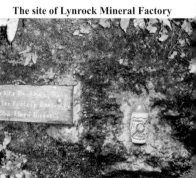

We fork right for 'Watersmeet' on a narrow path, threading our way through mature deciduous woodland to a second fork (29M). Here, bearing right downhill on the 'Riverside Walk', we cross a footbridge and turn left along an uneven river path, taking care on the slippery surface. Forty yards on we discover a pottery ginger beer bottle cemented into the rock face; a plaque identifies this as 'the site of the Lyn Rock Mineral Factory destroyed in the 1952 Flood disaster'.

The twisting rocky path follows the river then runs beside a high wooden fence before emerging into an open area and an arching stone bridge (42M); going left over **Chiselcombe** bridge then right, we arrive at the delightful **Watersmeet House**. This National Trust Tea Room and Information Point sitting at the confluence of **Hoaroak Water** and **East Lyn** was formerly a fishing lodge built in 1832 by the Halliday family. For a ¼ mile detour to **Hoaroak** waterfalls, cross the bridge to the right of the house, turning right then left up a flight of steps to the viewpoint and return the same way.

Continuing beside the house (45M) on the 'Fisherman's Path to Rockford', we climb gently away from the river to a fork (48M), veering sharp left uphill for 'Countisbury'. Rapidly gaining height, we soon look down on the grey roofs of **Watersmeet**, trudging our way up long zigzags between rocky outcrops; near the top the *sessile oaks* become more stunted and sparse and the zigzags shorten.

Rounding the shoulder into a clearing, we walk along a short ridge, forking left in front of a wall along 'Winston's path to Countisbury' (Wp.3 63M); stepping over a stile to leave the trees on a level contour path between gorse. Swinging gradually right round **South Hill Common**, splendid views open

up towards **Lynton**, across the valley to **Myrtleberry Cleave** and the moorland beyond. Dropping down to the top of a *combe* (Wp.4 72M) we keep right along the 'Countisbury off-road path' through a gate and along the field edge to a stile; the pavement beyond leads to **The Exmoor Sandpiper Inn**, where an all-day welcome is extended to children, dogs and muddy boots! Just beyond the inn (Wp.5 76M) and carefully crossing the A39 into a lane for 'Countisbury Church', we go through the churchyard to exit via a gate (Wp.6 79M) and turn left onto the cliff tops.

Here, greeted with wonderful views of **Lynton** and **Lynmouth**, acorn marked 'Coast path' signs guide us along a steadily descending path. This section includes some of Exmoor's finest coastal scenery; dropping down occasional flights of steps we pause to look back along stunning views of sandstone cliffs leading to **Foreland Point**. Passing a war time defence position our path gently rises before swinging right, resuming its gradual descent to a stile onto the **Countisbury Hill** road (Wp.7 104M).

Turning right downhill through a lay-by, we walk along the top of a bank next to the road, before bearing right down a winding path through woods to the seafront. A shelter on our left displays a mosaic depicting the bravery of the local lifeboat crew, after which we have an easy promenade through a pleasant park, retracing our steps across the white footbridge to the **Rhenish Tower** (Wp.8 121M).

A Magnificent Achievement

One stormy January night in 1899 **Countisbury Hill** presented one of the greatest challenges to the RNLI when the **Lynmouth** lifeboat crew answered a distress call from a vessel in difficulty off **Porlock**. The weather was so appalling that the oar propelled Louisa could not be launched from **Lynmouth,** so it was hauled on its heavy carriage for 14 miles up **Countisbury**'s 1:4½ gradient and down the even steeper **Porlock Hill**. This amazing feat involving 100 people and many horses took all night and after an immediate launch a successful rescue was secured.

This relaxing attractive walk offers us time to visit some of **Lynton's** Victorian influences including a water powered cliff railway and the North Walk promenade hewn out of the cliff face; even the Town Hall architecture evokes the 'Little Switzerland' image beloved by the Romantic poets.

After a village stroll we climb onto **Southcliffe** for a bird's eye view of the extraordinary rugged **Valley of Rocks** before descending to the dry valley floor past lovely coast views to **Lee Bay**.

We return along a dramatic section of coast on a gently undulating path designed to encourage **Lynton's** holiday makers to 'take the air' on their leisurely daily constitutional.

Access by bus: From **Barnstaple**, Nº309 and Nº310. From **Ilfracombe** and **Minehead Nº** 300.

Access by car: Lynton (SS 712495) lies just off the A39 on the B3234, 11 miles from both **Blackmoor Gate** and **Porlock**. Car parking in the village.

Short Walk

Fork right at Wp.3 into the **Valley of Rocks**, turn left along lane to rejoin at Wp.8. (2½ miles/4km, ascents & descents 125 metres)

Extension

Take the **Cliff Railway** or descend at Wp.10 to **Lynmouth** to start Walk 16. (10¼ miles/16½km, ascents & descents 550 metres)

Facing the Swiss chalet-style Town Hall (Wp.1 0M) we go left along **Lee Road** past several Victorian villas, most of which are now small hotels with pointed turrets and attic windows. Turning left into **Crossmead** against the one-way traffic system, we turn right at the T-junction into **Lydiate Lane**; where the main road veers left, our route climbs straight on up the lane. It's a steep pull with views back over the rooftops to **Foreland Point**; bearing right (Wp.2 10M) at a 'Lee Abbey & Bay' sign, our level tree covered track stays beside a neatly crafted stone-faced bank. At the 'Lee Abbey & Bay over Southcliffe' sign (Wp.3 12M) we fork left uphill with glimpses to **Hollerday Hill** and back to **Countisbury Hill**. For the

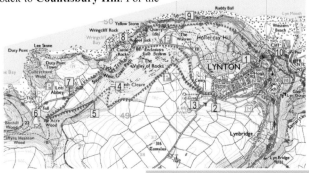

short walk, take the right fork downhill.

Now, climbing above the tree line we have our first sight of **The Valley of Rocks** with its knife-like jagged formation etched against the northern skyline; from right to left lie - **Hollerday Hill**, the small **Chimney Rock**, **Middle Gate**, **Rugged Jack** and finally, solitary **Castle Rock**. The steep valley slopes, covered in a natural cloak of gorse, bracken and scree surround the vivid emerald green of the Cricket Ground tucked 160 metres below on the valley floor. Gradually levelling, our grass path continues through gorse along the field edge; in front of us are the deep indentations of **Lee Bay** and **Woody Bay** with a backdrop of *hogs back cliffs* and the smooth profile of **Trentishoe Down**.

The view from Southcliffe over Lee Bay

Swinging right down a steep path above **Lee Abbey**, we head for a large rock marking a hairpin bend (Wp.4 37M); stepping around the rock, it's only a few paces to a viewpoint where we can fully appreciate the spectacle of this long dry valley.

The Valley of Rocks

Thousands of years ago the **Lyn River** flowed down the valley towards us before reaching the sea near **Lee Bay**. Two theories may account for the reason why the valley is now dry. One is that during the last Ice Age an ice shelf in the **Bristol Channel** pushed hard against the cliffs blocking **Lynmouth** and diverting the river down the coast along **The Valley of Rocks**. As the ice melted the **Lyn** re-established its current path. A second theory holds that the river originally flowed down the valley when sea levels were much lower; as climate change and rising sea levels led to significant coastal erosion the river found its current course and left the valley dry.

Retracing our steps to the large rock, we continue downhill through a gate into the grounds of **Lee Abbey Estate** (Wp.5 41M). Keeping right down the 'Lee Abbey' bridleway along the edge of the trees, we head past rocky outcrops to a track junction (Wp.6 48M), turning sharp right to the road by the abbey entrance (Wp.7 52M). For a ¼ mile detour to the beach at **Lee Bay**, go left down the road.

Pausing to enjoy a centuries-old April Fool's joke (see picture on the next page), we bear right along the lane past a Toll House; now, it's easy to see why this valley's sheer size and wild grandeur so captured the imagination of Victorian visitors.

We amble past the **Devil's Cheesewring**, its horizontal slabs of this craggy pillar

April Fool!

resembling a cider-press; 'cheese' is a local term for apple-pressing remains. The fingerpost pointing right to 'Mother Meldrum's cave' refers to a fictional wise woman in Lorna Doone who uses the rock to shelter from the elements; R D Blackmore is supposed to have based her on a local character.

Heading along the lane, we continue in driving instructor speak to... "go straight over the roundabout" ... past a 'goats grazing' sign to join the coast path to **Lynton** (Wp.8 64M).

Unexpectedly we emerge high above the sea onto a path carved into the cliff face; built in 1817 to cater for the perambulations of an expanding tourist market. Usually a herd of wild goats can be seen scrambling over the scree, chewing their way through vegetation.

Our twisting tarmac path undulates past rocky outcrops and salt-blasted trees to a path junction (Wp.9 74M) where we go straight on towards increasingly dramatic views of **Countisbury Hill** and **Foreland Point**'s distinctive promontory.

Now going into trees at the start of **North Walk** past hotels clinging to steep slopes, we cross a bridge over the **Cliff Railway** to a path junction (Wp.10 88M). The left hand path zigzags down to **Lynmouth** but we swing right up the lane to a T-junction, turning right onto the main street and Town Hall (Wp.11 93M).

The Cliff Railway

18 COUNTING THE COMBES TO COUNTISBURY

The most common word attached to Devon place names is *combe*, the Celtic word for valley and on this walk we encounter no less than six of them even including the double barrelled **Kipscombe Combe**. This wonderfully varied walk begins at **Countisbury Common** and crosses heath land and rolling pastures before returning along a splendid section of the coast path. In between we cross several *combes* falling steeply to the sea, including the intriguingly named **Pudleep Gurt**. With wide ranging views along the coast, inland vistas of Exmoor, mature woodlands and dramatic cliffs, this walk has it all. It even includes the option to be a mountain goat for half an hour, climbing the track from **Foreland Point**.

* if taking the main Adventurous Route
** at **The Exmoor Sandpiper Inn**, (5, if driving to **Lynton** or **Lynmouth**)

Access by car:
Our walk starts high above **Lynmouth** at the ancient burial ground of **Barna Barrow**. We park in the National Trust car park, 10 minutes from **Lynmouth** on the A39 near **Countisbury**. (SS 753496).

Access by bus:
Ilfracombe - **Minehead** bus N°300 passes the car park.

> **Extension**
> This walk can be joined with Walk 16 for a 13 mile/21 kilometre walk (ascents & descents 720 metres). From **Lynmouth** we follow Walk 16 to **Countisbury Churchyard** to join Walk 18 at Wp.19, going to Wp.20 then continuing from Wp.1 to Wp.19 where we leave Walk 18 and rejoin Walk 16 from the church and down **Countisbury Hill** to **Lynmouth**.

From the car park and facing the coast (Wp.1 0M), we take the right hand path (ENE) through level heathland, keeping right at the first fork. After 250 metres we join another path and bear right (Wp.2 4M ESE), continuing along the level path to cross a tarmac track (Wp.3 7M). Following the yellow waymark sign 'Kipscombe ½ mile', we go through a five-barred gate into a field, following the path and keeping the hedge on our left. We join a farm track (Wp.4 10M), continuing straight on for 60 yards with **Kipscombe Farm** on our left, and then turn right at the waymark sign and walk up the tarmac drive for 25 yards.

We turn left at the footpath sign, 'County Gate', onto the grass pasture. Coastal views appear as we gradually climb through the field, walking parallel to the bank on our left, to reach a gate in a wire fence (Wp.5 16M E). Walking straight ahead across the field, we reach a gap in a wire fence and keep on to another gate, following yellow waymarkings, with the field boundary wall to our left (Wp.6 22M). We soon reach a track and bear right, still with the stone wall on our left. Where the track curves right at the brow of the hill, we go through the five-barred gate ahead between two yellow waymarkings, into another pasture (ESE). The narrow path is well defined so we can enjoy the wide views of Exmoor as they open up. Dropping gently downhill alongside the wall, we reach the stile at the A39 (Wp.7 33M). Our route turns left to follow this busy main road for a short while, though as an alternative to walking along the road we cross over and climb up onto the *Devon Bank*, where we follow a narrow path along the top. After passing a minor road junction, the bank path widens, with yellow waymarkings on the fence posts. We continue alongside the A39 to reach a signpost marked 'Wingate Combe' (Wp.8 43M NE) and carefully re-cross the road to pass through a five-barred gate onto a permissive path.

In this sheep raising area, the track passes a holding area used to separate and count flocks, and also to make sure that each animal is wearing its personal identity tag. Continuing through two more five-barred gates, the track emerges into a field where we carry straight on, parallel to the stone wall, to reach the 'Wingate Combe and Coast Path' signpost beside a wood (Wp.9 49M). Turning left (NW), we enter a path between dark dense fir trees; if the mist is swirling at ground level it is easy to conjure up images of The Lord of the Rings. Emerging from the wood, we go over a stile straight ahead and head downhill, keeping the gorse bushes on our left. After 125 yards of walking on tussocky grass, and just beyond the metal field gate on the left, a footpath signpost points us downhill between the wall and gorse bushes. This steep path down **Wingate Combe** is very slippery and muddy in wet weather, so take it slowly. We go down through a pedestrian gate, following the narrow path through the trees as it zigzags back and forth across the stream.

Occasional splashes of yellow paint on stones and trees guide us until we reach the coast path sign with its distinctive acorn emblem (Wp.10 65M) where we go left for 'Countisbury' through mature deciduous oak woods and out into the open, an ideal picnic spot to recover from our scramble down the combe. After a short ascent we gradually descend to a pedestrian gate, entering National Trust woodland at **Glenthorne Cliffs**. (Wp.11 87M W).

The woodland at Wp.11

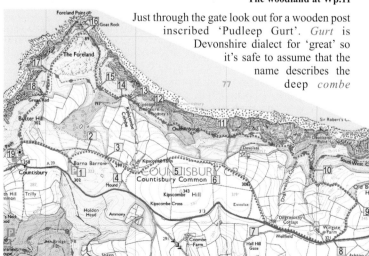

Just through the gate look out for a wooden post inscribed 'Pudleep Gurt'. *Gurt* is Devonshire dialect for 'great' so it's safe to assume that the name describes the deep *combe*

carving its way through the cliff to the sea. More *combes* follow as our path wanders through mature woods steadily down to **Swannel Combe** and then rising to **Chubbhill Combe**. (Wp.12 103M). There are several clearings where well positioned benches offer an opportunity to admire views of the coastline. Leaving **Glenthorne Cliffs**, we reach a stile by a tarmac track (Wp.13 108M) which we cross to continue ahead, following the coast path sign up the track to a junction with a tarmac road, where we turn right at the Lighthouse signpost (Wp.14 110M).

The scenery suddenly changes dramatically from green to grey as deciduous woodland gives way to bare, desolate scree-covered hills. Walking down the road (NW) into a broad deep valley, the sparse trees become increasingly smaller and stunted as the area becomes more exposed. Half way down the valley at **Coddow Combe** we reach a coast path signpost on our left to 'Countisbury'. (Wp.15 114M). At this point we have two options.

Easier Option
The recognised coast path rejoins our Lighthouse walk at Wp.17. This route is an easier option than our Lighthouse route, and should definitely be taken if walkers suffer from vertigo and/or the weather is inclement.

Main (Adventurous) Route

Foreland Lighthouse

However, for experienced adventurous walkers and in reasonable weather, continue down the tarmac road to **Foreland Lighthouse** (Wp.16 123M). This working lighthouse (1900) aids navigation in the **Bristol Channel** and was automated in 1994. **The Lighthouse Keepers' Cottage** is now run by the National Trust as holiday accommodation – the perfect spot for invigorating sea air and isolation!

Just before the lighthouse, we follow the footpath uphill to the left. This is an exposed narrow straight path which climbs steeply (SW) and is difficult underfoot, through several patches of loose scree, with the cliff sloping sharply away to the right. This is a slow section which requires concentration and several recovery stops, our exertions soon rewarded with magnificent far-reaching views of **Lynmouth** and **Lynton**.

As we reach the shoulder of the path having climbed up 115 metres, the coast path (our Easier Option) joins our track from the left hand side (Wp.17 148M). We walk up the broad coast path signed 'Countisbury' to the next signpost (Wp.18 153M), turning right to continue along the easier coast path which now follows the contour line, ignoring the sign to 'Barna Barrow'. First **Countisbury Hill** comes into view, then the church tower. At the top of the cliff is a signpost on our left marked 'Barna Barrow' (Wp.19 162M). We turn left for the final part of our route which takes us along a welcoming flat grassy track to the car park with spectacular inland views of Exmoor (Wp.1 171M).

To visit the church and/or **The Exmoor Sandpiper Inn**, take a right through the churchyard gate at Wp.19.

This circular route explores diverse countryside and the rugged coastline to the west of **Lynton**. Sir George Newnes, a Victorian publisher and local benefactor who owned a summer residence above the town funded several projects including the striking 'Little Switzerland' Town Hall. Our route passes two other Newnes projects; the amazing water powered **Cliff Railway** and narrow gauge railway are both still important tourist attractions.

The Valley of Rocks

After a steep climb out of **Lynton,** the inland leg to **Parracombe** is mainly along quiet lanes, then across fields into the wooded **Heddon Valley** before a climb onto the cliffs; our return offers two real 'wow' moments; a magnificent coastal section to **Woody Bay** and the weird and wonderful **Valley of Rocks**. Apart from the two climbs the rest of the route is comfortable walking; for a shorter walk, catch a bus to **Parracombe** perhaps visiting the two parish churches or **The Fox and Goose** before starting from Wp.7.

5	5H 8M	15 miles/24.1km		700m / 700m			4*

Shorter Linear walk	* in **Lynton, Parracombe, Heddon Valley**
Start from Wp.7 **Parracombe** (9.8 miles/15.8km, ascents 450 metres, descents 550 metres).	**Access by bus**: From **Barnstaple**, routes N°309 & N°310. From **Ilfracombe** and **Minehead** route N°300.
Alternative carriageway route between Hunter's Inn and Woody Bay Walk 1 from Wp.1 to Wp.6	**Access by car**: Lynton (SS 712495) lies just off the A39 on the B3234, 11 miles from both **Blackmoor Gate** and **Porlock**. Car parking in the village.

Facing the Town Hall (Wp.1 0M) we set off left along **Lee Road**, turning left into **Bellvue Avenue** towards 'Barnstaple' then right at a T-junction. Where the main road veers left (Wp.2 7M), we ignore a 'no through'road sign ahead to climb straight on up **Lydiate Lane**. Fortunately, this unremitting 15 minute steep slog rewards us with views of the **Valley of Rocks** to our right and behind, coastal scenes of **Countisbury Hill, Foreland Point** and the **Brecon Beacons**. Putting

The Toy Railway

From 1898 to 1935 a narrow gauge (1 foot 11½ inch) railway operated along a 19 mile 1:50 gradient line, connecting **Lynton** to the Southern Region network at **Barnstaple**. Sponsored by Sir George Newnes to attract tourists, there was talk of a viaduct across the **Valley of Rocks** to the Cliff Railway but this never materialised. Much of the track bed and bridges remain; **Woody Bay** station is the hub of an ambitious project to reinstate the line and trains now run along a mile of track.

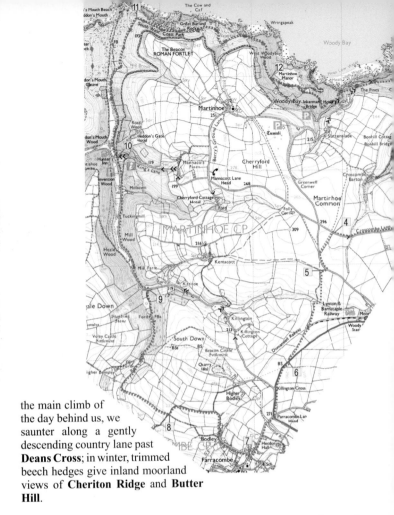

the main climb of the day behind us, we saunter along a gently descending country lane past **Deans Cross**; in winter, trimmed beech hedges give inland moorland views of **Cheriton Ridge** and **Butter Hill**.

Turning right at **Caffyns Cross** (Wp.3 45M) our easy walking continues; after passing a 'Croscombe Barton' bridleway the lane dips then climbs to the end of a hedge-bank where we turn left over a stile (Wp.4 73M) and follow a 'Footpath' pointer to the far side of a field. Going left along a road for 150 yards, and turning right into a field for 'Kemacott and Killington' we soon take a left hand gate on a 'Bridleway to A39' (Wp.5 79M), keeping near a hedge and heading downhill (S) over a stream and through a gate.

Bearing right uphill, our grass path swings left and right between gorse and the right hand hedge before going under a bridge. Keeping right into a field, we head diagonally away from the railway line (SSW) across two fields to the top left corner and the A39 (Wp.6 93M); there are lovely views to our right of **Trentishoe Down** and along the **Heddon Valley**. Here, turning right and taking care on a busy road, we ignore the first lane and continue along the verge to a Millennium Stone, bearing right down **Parracombe** lane to a crossroads (Wp.7 108M) - the start of the linear walk.

Our route turns right (0M) between attractive cottages on a lane for 'Bodley', then swings right up a 'Bridleway via Newbury lane'; climbing through an S-bend to a gate, we go ahead into a field on a 'West Hill Bridleway'.

Parracombe & Holwell Castle

There are views over medieval **Parracombe**, while to the right of a church tower is the mound of **Holwell Castle**, a fine example of a *motte and bailey* fortification; it's also possible to make out the lines of *lynchets* in

adjacent fields. Our sunken grass path goes through a second field then bends left down to a path crossroads (Wp.8 18M); turning right with a broken down hedgebank on our left, we stay beside field boundaries to reach a pedestrian gate.

An Exmoor gate latch

A delightful path curves down into the **Heddon Valley** between holiday cottages; now beside a pretty river tumbling over little rapids we stroll through woods along a tarmac lane; a short footpath diversion over a footbridge takes us through a glade and back onto the lane. Going left at a T-junction (Wp.9 44M) for four minutes, we can either take a left hand permissive path to **Hunter's Inn** through fields and woods, or continue along the lane through a deep wooded valley - beautiful all year round. Either way, we arrive in front of the Inn, open all day for food and a good pint; for picnickers there is a lovely spot ahead above **Heddon's Mouth**. Bearing right in front of the Inn (Wp.10 62M) for 25 yards, we swing left on a broad woodland track, forking left after a gate on a 'Heddon's Mouth Bridleway' (the **Alternative carriageway route** bears right).

Keeping left at the next fork beside the river and passing a stone bridge to a path junction, we bear right on the coast path for 'Woody Bay and Lynton', climbing a steep scree-covered slope to the headland above **Heddon's Mouth**

(Wp.11 89M). This is a super place to sit and absorb wonderful craggy views; eastwards the cream walls of **Lee Abbey** stand out against grey cliffs and the **Valley of Rocks**.

The coast path (between Wps. 11&12)

The gradient lessens, enabling us to stride out on a narrow well-defined path along the gorse and heather clad cliff side; rounding rocky outcrops we descend to a coastal waterfall, then enter a wood of gnarled *sessile oaks* above **Woody Bay** as our path sweeps gradually right, down to a gate (Wp.12 118M).

Going ahead down a rough tarmac track, then bearing right for 'Lynton' and Russia - you'll see what we mean - along a wide path, we turn left onto the **Lynton Toll Road**.

Bowling steadily downhill, we keep right onto a path (Wp13 142 M) for 'Lee Abbey and Bay' and after a short climb curve gradually right through trees to a path junction above a stream. Going right, then immediately left down a narrow 'Lynton' path across a footbridge, we bear left onto a broad 'Lee Abbey and Lynton' track. Winding around woodland contours to a Y-junction, we fork left to rejoin the Toll Road at **Lee Abbey** (Wp.14 161M). Bearing right along the lane past a Toll House - no charge for us - we step into the spectacular **Valley of Rocks**, to our right the 160 metre high slope of **South Cleave** plunges to the dry valley floor, whilst seaward, a line of jagged peaks protect the valley. Heading along the lane past **Castle Rock**, our route crosses a roundabout and at a 'goats grazing' sign joins the coast path to **Lynton** (Wp.15 173M).

Emerging high above the sea our twisting tarmac path undulates past rocky outcrops along the cliff side; groups of wild goats can often be seen picking their way over the scree, grazing on pockets of sparse vegetation. Our final dramatic coastal views are to the **Foreland** before heading into trees at the start of **North Walk** past houses and hotels precariously perched on steep slopes; crossing a bridge over the **Cliff Railway** and continuing up the lane to a T-junction we turn right to the Town Hall (Wp.16 200M).

20 ROBBER'S BRIDGE, PORLOCK WEIR, CULBONE & BROOMSTREET FARM

Contrary to any villainous connotations conjured up by its name, **Robber's Bridge** is an idyllic and peaceful setting from which we start this marvellous walk. Much of it follows ancient broad tracks through broad-leaved woodland, along the spectacular coast and across high open moor. The beauty of these tracks is that we can strike up a rhythm and also walk side by side.

The outward section climbs out of a valley, then descends through woods to the pretty seaside hamlet of **Porlock Weir**. The middle part along the **South West Coast Path** offers a real sense of remoteness and centuries of unchanging landscape. Finally, after a steep but mercifully short ascent onto **North Moor**, there are splendid inland views before the descent to **Oare Water** and **Robber's Bridge**. As well as enjoying these natural beauties, we pass the highest Free House on Exmoor, see the medieval **Culbone Stone**, and visit England's smallest parish church.

4/5   4H   12½ miles/20km   575m / 575m   3*

* **Anchor Hotel** and **Ship Inn** (food all year), **Culbone Inn** (food Easter-Oct)

A slightly shorter and easier return - along country lanes can be completed by turning left onto the tarmac lane before **Silcombe Farm** (SS835482). Continue for a mile then take the first right to **The Culbone Inn** at Wp.3 and back down **Met Combe** (11½ miles/18.4km).	**Access by car:** reach **Robber's Bridge** car park (SS 820464) from the A39 near **County Gate**, signposted 'Malmsmead and Oare', turning left at **Oare Church**. **Access by bus:** DevonBus Nº300 to **Culbone Inn** on A39 and join the walk at Wp.3.

From the car park (Wp.1 0M) we walk along the road towards the bridge, turning right onto a bridleway signed 'Culbone Inn'. We go through the gate then right up a delightful broad track (ENE), steadily climbing out of the valley with increasingly grand views of the U-shaped valley below. The gradient eases as the track swings left into the smaller side valley of **Met Combe**; light trees, heather and bracken cover the slopes, and looking back we can see across the heart of Exmoor.

We've almost completed the climb when we reach a metal field gate on our left by a stand of beech trees (Wp.2 15M), then continue through a gate just below **Culbone Inn**. We follow the signpost marked 'Bridleway A39 Road' to the main road (Wp.3 22M) which we cross with care, onto a minor road to walk to the brow of the hill. Just beyond the cattle grid on our left is a stile and sign pointing the way to the 'Culbone Stone' (Wp.4 25M). It's an easy 10 minute stroll into the wood to visit this little pointed mediaeval stone engraved with what looks like a magnifying glass.

Back at the stile (35M) we go left down the road to reach a gate on our right (Wp.5 38M) signed 'Bridleway to Porlock Weir' (ESE). Entering the wooded **Smallacombe**, we drop down the track, cross the stream (Wp.6 45M) and bear left down the valley. At a signpost by **Pitt Farm**, we turn left for **Porlock Weir** (Wp.7 52M) past the house to enter a narrow tarmac lane which soon joins the **Worthy Toll Road** signposted 'Porlock Weir'. Leaving the road a few minutes later at a sign to **Porlock Weir**, we turn right onto a woodland track, crossing the stream to arrive at a path junction (Wp.8 62M) where we go straight on at the 'Porlock Wier' (sic) signpost, gently rising through woodland until the track levels out.

Ten minutes later (passing another 'Porlock Wier' sign) we go straight on towards **Porlock Ford**, then down a steepening track. Ahead, we glimpse **Porlock Bay**, and as a track joins from the right, we turn sharp left (Wp.9 78M), continuing down this pleasant track to the bottom of the hill to a junction with the coast path (Wp.10 91M). We go left for a few paces, then left again onto the road.

Porlock Bay

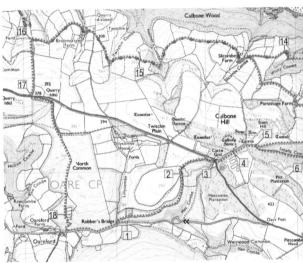

Where the road forks we head left along the lane (NW), past a thatched summer house and the white painted **Saint Nicholas Church**. Enjoying beautiful views across the bay, we pass a row of stone cottages and turn right down a side road for a few yards to arrive at the pebble beach of **Porlock Weir** (Wp.11 100M), a good spot for a break, with benches to enjoy a picnic, near **The Ship Inn** and **Anchor Hotel**.

Our walk restarts between these two buildings (0M) as we rejoin the coast path marked 'Culbone Church 2½ miles'. We have an easy stroll along field edges then onto a track which rises through a field gate to join a lane. We turn right past **Worthy Manor** to reach **Worthy Toll House** (8M) and admire the thatched stone walled building (see the picture on the following page).

Following the coast path, we strike uphill through two short tunnels, part of the landscaped gardens of the now demolished **Ashley Combe Mansion**. The original coast path is blocked by a landslide, and a permissive path takes us zigzagging up the hillside. As the path levels, we find a beautifully crafted curved stone seat tucked into the dry stone wall.

We tramp on uphill on a broad track following the occasional sign for 'Culbone Church'. The undulating, twisting track through deciduous woods, including *sessile oaks*, reaches a signpost marked 'Culbone Church' (Wp.12 27M) before curving inland and gradually descending to the isolated settlement of **Culbone**. Just beyond the house with the archway, we turn right at the signpost for 'Church and footpath to Silcombe' through the churchyard (Wp.13 40M) (yet another misspelt 'Porlock Wier' direction sign).

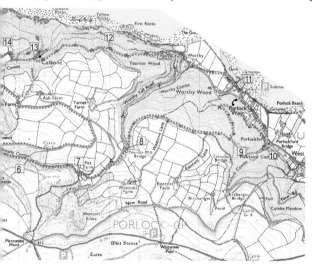

We enter **St Beuno's** churchyard to visit its tiny but perfectly formed ancient church. With our backs to the church door, we go straight across the churchyard to exit via a gate turning right to **County Gate**, **Silcombe**.

After a steep ascent up a pretty *combe*, we bear right to rejoin the coast path at the edge of the wood (Wp.14 51M) (our last mispelt sign!) and our route takes us left up the track towards **Broomstreet** and **Lynmouth**, uphill and through a field gate to reach a tarmac lane. The shorter route is to our left, but we go ahead, towards the imposing grey stone farm buildings of **Silcombe**. We swing right and up past the farmhouse (1866) as the lane reverts to a farm track running between the fields all the way to **Broomstreet Farm**.

It's pleasant walking between *Devon banks* and hedges with frequent coastal views, till we swing inland round **Holmer's Combe** to reach a five-barred track gate adjacent to a gate marked 'Twitchen' (Wp.15 77M). We continue along the track, skirting the open aspects of **Twitchen Combe** with its many remnants of stone walls and hedgerows. As a track joins on our left we go straight on to **Broomstreet Farm**, signposted 'Bridleway County Gate', dropping down past an impressive solid farm and keeping right towards **County Gate** along the grassy way, through several fields and gates with more clear views of the **Bristol Channel**.

We leave the coast path at a four-way signpost (Wp.16 97M), going left (S) signed 'Bridleway Oareford' to climb steeply up over the hill beside the wire fence, through a gate and on upwards. It's hard work, but the excellent views along the coast are worth the exertion, and an Exmoor panorama is revealed at the hilltop as we arrive at a gate onto the A39 road (Wp.17 109M). Crossing the road, we turn left, bearing right after 100 yards along a track for 'Bridleway Oareford', through the gate and onto the open moorland beyond. We follow the track round the top of **Deddycombe** to the corner of the fence on our left where a signpost directs us to continue straight on across the moor to **Oareford** (S).

The track gradually descends and curves right among the heather.

As it narrows we look for blue-tipped post markers and aim for the right hand edge of the trees, then head down to the pedestrian gate (Wp.18 127M).

Beech trees near Wp.18

After enjoying splendid views of **Chalk Water**, we set off down a steeply wending path to a pedestrian footbridge where we keep left to join the lane, and left again beside the river on our return to the tranquil setting of **Robber's Bridge** (Wp.19 141M).

Our linear route starts from **Wheddon Cross**, gradually climbing pastures to **Lype Hill** and a magnificent panorama of the **Brendon Hills** before dropping steeply into the **Luxborough Valley**. Here, a lane leads us to an atmospheric path running along a hidden valley through the ivy covered ruins of a forgotten village. The intriguing mysterious settlement of **Clicket**, complete with houses, lime kiln, mill and tiny footbridges, was abandoned in the 19th century but little is known about its history.

When walking this route for the first time, we felt like 19th century explorers and it still provides a frisson of excitement.

Continuing to pretty **Timberscombe** our final leg is over a common and along a wooded coach road to **Dunster**. On a practical note, some of the **Brendon Hills** paths on the OS map are not the same as on the ground, but this book, plus blue painted blobs and arrows guide us through.

4	3H 50M	11.1 miles/17.8km	390m 630m	3*

Shorter route	* at **Wheddon Cross, Timberscombe, Dunster**
To **Timberscombe** Wp.11 (8 miles/12.8km ascents 230 metres, descents 450 metres). N°398 bus to **Dunster**.	**Access by bus:** First bus N°398 connects **Minehead-Dunster-Wheddon Cross- Dulverton** and **Tiverton. Dunster**'s bus stop is in the **High Street**.

Access by car: **Dunster** is 3 miles from **Minehead** on the A396; ½ mile from the junction with A39. Park in the car park by the Information Centre (SS 993439). In **Wheddon Cross** the car park (SS 924388) is next to **The Rest and Be Thankful Inn**.

Turning left from **Wheddon Cross** car park (Wp.1 0M) along the A396 we bear right at the War Memorial, then right again at a 'Putham' fork, gently ascending a tree banked lane.

Lambing season on the Brendon Hills

Going right up a blue tipped 'Luxborough' bridleway (Wp.2 7M) we steadily climb a rough track then on through two fields beside a left hedge to a gate ahead. Going left and right through a high deer gate (Wp.3 21M) and straight on past **Pitleigh Kennels** to the far side of a field, we take the right hand gate then follow the left hand fence. Gradually climbing **White Moor**, we go left along a mature beech hedge to a gate (Wp.4 38M) then turn right across a pasture, aiming slightly left for a gate in the far hedge.

Crossing a lane and still on the 'Luxborough' bridleway we go diagonally left to a fence corner, continuing ahead through a gate left of **Lype Hill** trig point (Wp.5 50M 423 metres). Views that have been improving during our climb are now truly lovely with a panorama of moor, sea and pastures; the wildlife is abundant and you may have the luck to see deer, hares and buzzards.

From the summit we gently descend (ESE) beside a right hand fence, going through a gate then bearing left (E) across a field under electricity cables to a gate in the middle of a fence (Wp.6 57M). Here a 'Luxborough' fingerpost and blue blobs point us straight on through two more fields, picking up the fence line then bend left to a gate (Wp.7 64M). Entering the last field we gradually bear left to a field corner walking towards a rolling woodland landscape and the distant **Quantock Hills**.

We go left down a red earth track (NNE) for 'Luxborough', our route descending steeply and becoming a narrow sunken lane, often wet after rain; at a field gate we pause for a helicopter view of **Churchtown** and the **Luxborough Valley**.

A helicopter view of Churchtown

Our rapid descent continues beside a left bank as we swing left to a gate then bear right down a track and over a railway sleeper footbridge. We take a 'Bridleway' gate ahead and climb an enclosed path to a lane (Wp8 90M) - **St Mary's Church** (Walk 22) is 3 minutes to our right. Leaving **Churchtown**, we turn left up a lane to **Beech Tree Cross** and a fine lunch-time bench. After bearing right along a **Dunster** lane, we descend past **Nurcott Farm** and a huge Monkey Puzzle tree, leaving the road just after a cottage on a yellow marked left hand 'Clicket and Timberscombe' footpath (Wp9 101M).

Always keeping the small river on our right between here and **Timberscombe**, our footpath switches between the side and floor of a valley, crossing several tributaries. It's a delightful section as we gently descend between fern strewn banks and a tiny stream past the ruins of a kiln where lime was made to improve the soil; it must have been a tough life scratching out an existence in the damp surroundings.

After crossing a stile, we head over a field into rough woodland and through a gate, dropping steadily across the slope to find ivy covered tumble-down walls and to our left, a static deer (Wp10 119M), the first of several metal sculptures of animals and birds dotted in the woods - look out for the fan-tailed capercaillie, a long way from home.

Strolling along this quiet hidden valley we arrive at an ancient hedge-bank where a black metal boar peers out from the undergrowth; after crossing a streamlet our path drops to a signpost beside the river.

Our route goes straight on, but this is a lovely place to explore; on our right is a dinky bridge crossing what would probably have been a *leat*, while over a stile there are more ruins including a mill-stone lying on the ground - the 1891 OS map records this spot as 'Beckham Mill - disused'.

The dinky bridge at Clicket

Going straight on and forking right at a path junction, we climb a stile, crossing the slope of a steep pasture to a hunting gate. Wending our way through woodland dells shimmering with bluebells, we bear left onto a track for 50 yards then go right back onto our path, dropping to a signpost on the river bank (135M); we've apparently come from 'Beach Tree Cross' (sic).

Our undulating path twists and turns through gates and over stiles along a widening valley before eventually becoming a track; turning right on a road, we stride past the red stone of **St Petrocks's Church** into **Timberscombe**'s village square (Wp.11 157M). Turning right beside **The Lion Inn** and immediately right along **Brook Street** to a junction, we go left uphill on a blue marked 'Dunster and Luxborough Bridleway' to the end of a post and rail fence and

Timberscombe

turn right through a gate.

Climbing a rough track and bending left for 'Dunster' we pass farm outbuildings, continuing beside a left hedge and through gates into a large field at the brow of a hill. Going straight ahead (E) with a copse on our right, we gently bear right (ESE) along a bracken field edge taking a blue marked path through a gate (Wp.12 175M) into a fir wood.

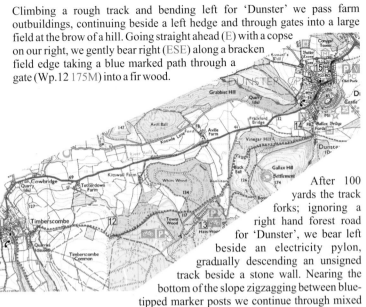

After 100 yards the track forks; ignoring a right hand forest road for 'Dunster', we bear left beside an electricity pylon, gradually descending an unsigned track beside a stone wall. Nearing the bottom of the slope zigzagging between blue-tipped marker posts we continue through mixed deciduous woodland to a track junction. Continuing ahead on a level 'A396 Footpath' for 100 yards, the path swings left; we go straight on past a wooden vehicle barrier and turn left onto a lane (Wp.13 191M).

After pottering down beside the quaintly named **Nutcombe Bottom** picnic area, a lane joins from our right; 50 yards further on we bear right, climbing a path up **Vinegar Hill** through rhododendron thickets and around the contours to a broader track at the crest. Descending left along an old coach road towards **Dunster** with glimpses of the village and castle, we go straight on at a track junction (Wp14 215M) to cross picturesque **Gallox Bridge.** Walking between the cottages we turn right into **Mill Gardens** then left beside a *leat* up to a road T-junction; bearing right and ambling along cobbled pavements we pass **St. George's Church** and **Yarn Market** (Wp.15 227M) to return to the car park. (230M).

Luxborough is set in a broad fertile valley, protected by the ridge of the **Brendon Hills**, comprising of the three hamlets of **Churchtown**, **Kingsbridge** and **Pooltown**. This is part of Exmoor's gentler landscape; the valley floor and rolling slopes are covered with a patchwork of fields, gradually giving way to woods and heath land on the rounded hill tops.

Our route sets off from the peaceful valley along grass tracks and sunken lanes, climbing onto **Withycombe Common** to enjoy views along the **Somerset** coast and the beauty of the **Quantock** and **Brendon Hills**. Our return down a steep hill takes us back to the pretty village with time to explore an ancient church and enjoy the benefits of the local hostelry.

2 | **2 H** | 5¾ miles/9¼km | 325m / 325m | **3** *

* The Royal Oak Inn (food all year)

Stroll
Follow the route to Wp.4 then continue straight along the lane to **Luxborough** (2 miles/3.2km).

Access by car: Luxborough is 7 miles east of **Wheddon Cross**, signed from the B3224 on the Brendon Hills. Access from **Timberscombe** via a minor road to **Couple Cross** signed to **Luxborough**. The car park is beside the Village Hall (SS 985377).

Access by bus: From **Minehead** on Wednesday and Friday, limited service on Webberbus Nº564

... beneath a beech canopy ...

Turning right from the car park (Wp.1 0M) we stroll along the road by the stone-clad **Millennium Village Hall**, passing several honeysuckle covered cottages and the attractive gardens of **Luxborough Tea Rooms**.

Crossing the stone bridge over the **Washford River**, we turn immediately right (Wp.2 4M) onto a path heading gently uphill beneath a beech canopy, before swinging left downhill beside a stream.

Continuing up the valley through mixed woodland we pass a stone cottage, bearing right at a track fork (Wp.3 17M) along a narrow tree lined path; beyond another cottage we turn right onto a lane towards the hamlet of **Churchtown**. At a T-junction beside the high stone wall of **Butchers Farm** we go right for 100 yards, then left up the 'Monkham Hill' tarmac track (Wp.4 26M). To visit the interesting 12th century **Church of St Mary's** we go left beside **Church Cottage**.

Climbing steadily between **Church Cottage** and **The Parsonage** into a grassy sunken lane, our views are obscured by tall fern covered banks until we

reach the first field gate; now spread out before us is a mix of ploughed fields, grass pastures and woods creating a mosaic of green, red and yellow.

Our track levels, then goes downhill bearing left to a metal gate on our left; (Wp.5 43M) we go through down a wide earth track curving right across **Perley Combe** to a gate beyond the stream.

Continuing beside the woodland edge, we turn left at a path crossroads (Wp.6 50M) up a steep forest track through the managed **Dunster** woodlands to a 5-way signpost (Wp.7 61M).

We follow the 'Rodhuish' track, the second on our right. Our route heads over heath (ENE) past **Withycombe Common** trig point (381 metres); this is comfortable easy walking, with views over **Bridgwater Bay** from **Blue Anchor** to **Watchet** and beyond to **Hinckley Point Power Station**. Soon after, the **Quantock Hills** come into view ahead; where the track swings sharply left, (Wp.8 71M) we turn right on a narrower path marked with a splash of blue paint on a piece of slate.

Strolling (SE) on a level earth bridleway between fields and light woodland, we enjoy extensive views of the broad valley dotted with villages against a backdrop of the **Quantock Ridge** and **Brendon Hills**. At a bridleway junction we go through a gate for 'Luxborough' (Wp.9 81M) keeping to the level ground straight across the field (S) to a gate in the far hedge, pausing here to admire last views of the superb patchwork of fields (see picture on the next page).

We follow the curving track to descend the steepening hill

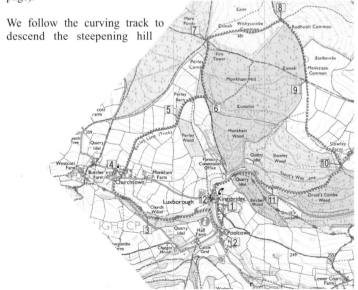

A patchwork of fields

beside the left hedge, then bear right through a gate above **Slowley Farm**, before dropping between mature oaks through a gate and onto a lane (Wp.10 96M).

Now we turn right for 150 yards to a wide clearing, where we go left on a forest track for a steady descent.

We head straight down, ignoring other tracks on our left, onto a smaller grass path, to turn right by a house entrance along a gravel track (Wp.11 108M).

Crossing the bridge to a T-junction we turn right along the lane beside the river, past the mill to **Luxborough** and the welcoming **Royal Oak Inn** (Wp.12 119M).

The ancient Church of St Mary's, Churchtown

Set in this tranquil location since at least the 12th century the church tower has an unusual *saddleback* roof; the churchyard boasts an early cross of either Saxon or Norman origin, and two 15th century tombs decorated with panelled sides and shields.

Inside, an old wooden barrelled roof covers the chancel and a 13th century font, contrasting with a colourful Millennium stained glass window.

Much of the northern slopes of the **Brendon Hills** are covered with coniferous woods managed with support from **The Forestry Commission**; wide trails offer comfortable sheltered walking cutting across steep gradients into deep valleys. Hidden in the woods, we discover remnants of the amazing Victorian ingenuity used to resolve a transportation problem; how to move tons of iron ore from top to bottom of the ridge. In a valley floor we stroll along a disused railway line before climbing out of the woods through pastures onto the ridge; there are terrific far-reaching views on this final section across northern Exmoor and the **Somerset** coast.

Access by car: **Ralegh's Cross** is 9 miles east of **Wheddon Cross** on the B3224 at the junction with the B3190 from **Bampton** to **Washford**. Park in lay-by (ST 035344) ¼ mile west of the inn.

The view from Wp.2

From the lay-by (Wp.1 0M), we walk along the busy road from **Ralegh's Cross** towards **Wheddon Cross** and turn right through a double gate (Wp.2 5M); a small 'Roadwater' permitted footpath sign tucked into the hedge points us down a stony track between the fields.

The Comberow Incline

Two railway tracks ran ¾ mile from a winding tower on top of the **Brendon Ridge** straight down a 1:4 gradient to the valley floor at **Comberow**; a drop of 230 metres. Black and white photographs clearly show a vivid scar running down the steep hillside. Wagons filled with iron ore mined on the ridge were hauled up and down using a pulley system, joining the West **Somerset Mineral Railway** to **Watchet Harbour**. We can still wonder at the scale of this undertaking and the number of man hours required to blast through rock and build earth embankments. There's an evocative photographic display in **Ralegh's Cross Inn**.

On entering a plantation with its beech fringe, the distant views disappear as we go straight on down the main earth track, gradually curving left and enjoying comfortable walking between tall firs trees to a signed 'footpath' junction (Wp.3 15M). Turning left uphill, our narrow path bears right after 25 yards to cross a stream, then climbs a short way before we descend over another stream to suddenly step onto a man-made slope (Wp.4 18M). Today the incline is overgrown, but you can still imagine how this Victorian engineering feat might have looked in its heyday.

Bearing right to a path junction and ignoring the right hand 'public footpath' sign, we turn left uphill for a short distance then swing right beside a mature beech hedge where our broad track resumes its descent. Ignoring another yellow 'footpath' sign on our right, we continue steadily downhill to a path T-junction (Wp.5 30M) going left for 'Roadwater via Comberow' along the valley floor; coming out of the trees we are faced with a towering hillside packed with enormous firs.

Rounding a *combe*, a waterfall on our left drops down a rock face; impressive in winter, it's a trickle during dry weather. After a short muddy section the track splits and we take the right fork heading gently uphill, then bearing left up a tree choked *combe*; the trees encroach and our path gets narrower as we swing right over a stream past a derelict cottage.

Turning right for (Wp.6 43M) 'Roadwater via Comberow', we head steadily down the side of a *combe* along a fern lined path and ignoring a yellow-marked right hand turning, continue ahead on a small path keeping the stream on our right. Clambering over the odd fallen tree in this unkempt wilderness and squelching through a few wet bits beside the bank, our path gently climbs and dries out to reach a path junction (Wp.7 57M). Bearing right downhill for 'Comberow' our path bends right then runs downhill along the woodland edge to the valley floor, crossing a bridge to a track junction. We are now at the foot of the incline at **Comberow** where the railway ran down the valley to **Watchet**; the station and sidings are long gone but some of the Station Master's house still stands.

Turning sharp left (Wp.8 62M) on a 'Roadwater' track, we head down beside the stream and through a gate; now on the bed of the railway, the next mile is easy woodland walking along the valley floor. Passing a pretty stone cottage and garden the trees disappear for a few moments before we reach the edge of **Pit Wood** on the right slope. Turning right off the line for 'Chidgley' opposite the entrance to **Pit Mill** (Wp.9 81M), we climb steadily up a pine forest trail, bending left to a junction then right on a blue marked 'Sticklepath' track (Wp.10 86M).

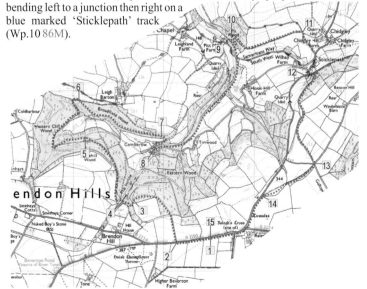

Looking back from Wp.11

Climbing to a gate, we emerge from our sylvan trek onto an open path along the side of a steep valley; the gradient eases as we stroll under overhanging beech branches and through a gate in the hedge (Wp.11 99M), turning immediately right along a track. Watching out for traffic, we go right up the road around a shallow S-bend, crossing over before the next right bend to turn left on a 'Monksilver and Ralegh's Cross' track (Wp.12 107M).

Forking right at a junction for 'Ralegh's Cross', our path climbs between mature trees, going through a gate beside a left hand bank.

As the trees thin on our right our efforts are rewarded with a panorama stretching from **Brendon Ridge** to **Dunkery Beacon**, across the patchwork quilt slopes of **Luxborough Valley** to the coast; looking south west the incline summit is just visible above the tree line.

Fine views from Brendon Ridge

There's a lovely picnic spot before the next gate; we sat one afternoon in early October watching a herd of twenty or so red deer in the fields below escorted by a fine stag, while buzzards spiralled upwards on the thermals.

Curving up beside a hedge through rough pastures to a crest, we head slightly down to a gate at a road corner; on the OS map the section straight ahead has the fantastic name of **Galloping Bottom Lane**! Our more sedate route is right through the second metal gate marked 'Ralegh's Cross' (Wp.13 128M); strolling through a long narrow field to a gate at the far end, we bear slightly left, following the line of the left hand hedge to a road (Wp.14 137M). Going left along the ridge road and using the grass verge when necessary, we swing right past **Ralegh's Cross Inn**, enjoying final sweeping views before returning to our start point (Wp.15 146M).

24 HAWKRIDGE CIRCULAR via ANSTEY GATE

Exmoor's southern fringe west of **Dulverton** may be less frequented by hikers; nonetheless, it provides good walking and a wide variety of countryside and scenery. This half day stroll offers a perfect Exmoor taster; a blend of fields, rough pastures, streams, open moors and woods, plus sightings of red deer and ponies - it's Exmoor in miniature.

Our route from the quiet hilltop village of **Hawkridge** heads through fields with views to **Winsford Hill**, before climbing a lane to **Tarr Post**. Descending over rough pastures to pretty **Dane's Brook**, we climb to a ridge road at **Anstey Gate**, looking across Devon's rolling hills; then, strolling down **Anstey Rhiney Moor** into woodland, we re-cross **Dane's Brook** before a short steep climb to **Hawkridge**.

Shorter walk	
The Access Land either side of the ridge road along **Molland** and **Anstey Commons** gives plenty of opportunities for shorter walks.	**Access by car**: Take a signed lane off B3222 just south of **Dulverton** play area; follow 'Hawkridge' signs west for 5 miles. Park in the lay-by (SS 860307) near the village hall.

Extension
Join with Walk 32 for an 11.1 mile/17.8km figure of eight walk (ascents & descents 620 metres).

From the lay-by we set off to a T-junction (Wp.1 0M) by a telephone box, turning left along the 'Withypool' lane for 100 yards; at a yellow-marked 'Footpath to Tarr Steps' sign, we bear right up wooden steps and through a gate. Crossing the stile ahead, we stroll through three fields, going diagonally left (N); our path gradually descends through a metal gate, then a gap in the next hedge, before swinging down to a stile in the far right hand corner (Wp.2 9M).

Strolling through fields after Wp.1

On our right are views into the wooded **Barle Valley** and along the skyline lies the long open ridge of **Winsford Hill**. Walking just above and parallel to a right hand bank, we continue straight on where it bends right; going through a gateway, then over a field, to a gate at the bottom of a pasture (Wp.3 16M). Turning left up a quiet country lane to a T-junction at **Tarr Post**, we bear left for 50 yards, then right through a double gate (Wp.4 30M) onto a track; a small blue tipped 'Bridleway & Footpath' sign is tucked in beside the left hedge.

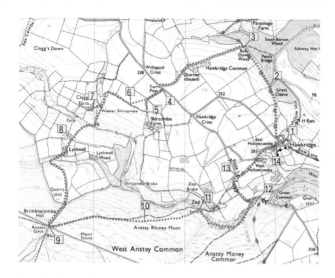

Broad views of **Anstey Common** stretch across the horizon as we gently descend to the point where the track starts bearing left; here going through a gate on our right (Wp.5 33M), a low wooden permitted path sign allows us to go diagonally left over a field to a gate in the hedge (Wp.6 35M). Turning right through the gate and strolling beside the hedge to a small valley, we swing left between bracken on a path running down to a sign post (Wp.7 41M).

The footbridge over Dane's Brook

Following the 'Anstey Gate' footpath, we descend beside a field edge to cross a raised wooden footbridge over **Dane's Brook**; its course marks a county boundary from Somerset into Devon. This quiet area of rough pastures and light woodland is frequented by red deer, especially in autumn during the rutting season; a good time to see them is early morning or late afternoon.

Deer country above Dane's Brook

During our research it was here that we got closest to a magnificent stag; clearly observed through binoculars but not quite close enough for a good photo. What was clear however, was the stag's extraordinary deep guttural bellowing as he protected his hinds.

Turning right along the bank, then left up a track, we climb through rough pasture past a solitary tree, following a low grass mound up to the tree line

(Wp.8 52M); going through a gate, a roughly painted yellow arrow points us left to the brow of a hill. With the buildings of **Lyshwell Farm** on our right, we join a track, curving right through a gate onto a lane, to descend into a small bracken-filled *combe*; now a long steady climb takes us up a lane through moorland pasture past a cattle grid to **Anstey Gate** (356 metres). A ridge road runs from **Molland Common** on our right, over **West** and **East Anstey Commons**, down to **Dulverton**, giving splendid views of central Devon's rolling landscape; there is an interesting bench near the cattle grid, a peaceful spot to rest and enjoy the scenery.

Taking the 'Hawkridge Bridleway' we go left through a gate beside the cattle grid (Wp.9 70M), and re-cross the road onto grassy moorland; ignoring the track parallel to the road, we go diagonally right, ambling gradually downhill in a fairly straight line, aiming for the far V of a valley floor.

After 6 minutes our track splits; keeping right, we reach a large grass circle half way down the common (Wp.10 82M); there are pleasant views across the valley to **Shercombe Brake**, while ahead rich bracken colours flow into the autumnal hues of the tree canopy. Continuing in the same downhill direction (E) towards the valley V, our route goes through gorse clumps; the main path is discernible, but several paths criss-cross this Access Land, so if in doubt, keep forking left at junctions, downhill across the slope.

Entering thicker gorse and light woodland, we pick our way down a stony eroded path to a signpost on the stream bank (Wp.11 92M); keeping the water on our left and bearing right to 'Slade Bridge', we climb a few yards onto a path beneath low overhanging branches. Crossing a small tributary, our undulating path meanders beside a pretty section of stream; as **Slade Bridge** comes into view below and the path starts to climb, we fork left on a smaller path, dropping to the bank and bridge. However, if like us you miss this fork, simply follow the uphill path, beyond the bridge onto a lane and turn left downhill.

Crossing **Dane's Brook** (Wp.12 106M) to re-enter Somerset, we climb steeply up a lane and turn right through a gate on a bridleway for 'Hawkridge' (Wp.13 114M); going up a field over the crest we keep left of a house with tall chimneys to a corner gate. Bearing right, we pass a beautiful **Hawkridge** seat adorned with carvings of a red deer and buzzard, before strolling along the lane to finish our walk (Wp.14 122M).

The carved Hawkridge seat

25 DULVERTON, HINAM CROSS & THE BARLE VALLEY

The bustling market town of **Dulverton** located in the beautiful **Barle Valley** on the southern boundary of the National Park is an enjoyable place to visit, boasting a number of interesting shops, cafés and pubs; the **Exmoor National Park Visitors' Centre** in **Fore Street** has an exhibition and local information.

Our countryside route climbs out of the **Barle Valley** through pastures, rolling hills and a quiet beech lined lane to **Hinam Cross**; returning to the valley, we explore an Iron Age hilltop settlement at **Brewer's Castle** before a riverside stroll through woods to **Marsh Bridge** and back to **Dulverton**. This walk provides year round interest; in spring field banks are covered with wild flowers, while in autumn, beech leaves create a tapestry of rich colours. The character of the **Barle** also changes with the seasons, an unhurried sparkling summer river becomes charged with muddy foaming water in winter spate. GPS reception is intermittent from Wp.8 along a well used track to the road at **Marsh Bridge**.

3 · 2½ H · 6.7 miles/10.8km · 320m / 320m · 4*

Shorter Walk
From Wp.4 turn right off the lane down a 'Permitted Path' to a wood, bearing left along its edge to a road, then right to Wp.13 (3.2 miles/5.2km, ascents & descents 140 metres).

Extension
Walk to Wp.12 and turn left over **Marsh Bridge** joining Walk 26 at Wp.4 (7.7 miles/12.4 km, ascents & descents 410 metres).

*Dulverton

Access by bus: First bus N°307 from **Barnstaple** and **Taunton**; First bus N°398 from **Tiverton** and **Minehead**.

Access by car: **Dulverton** is on the B 3222, 2 miles off the A396 connecting **Tiverton** (13 miles) and **Minehead** (19 miles). It is 10 miles from **Exford** on the B3223. Car parks are in the town centre and by the river.

Starting from the riverside car park beside Lorna Doone's statue (Wp.1 0M, see the picture on the next page), we head to the bridge, crossing the **River Barle** and turning immediately right up a lane, then bearing right on a 'public footpath' between mossy banks to a track junction (Wp.2 5M).

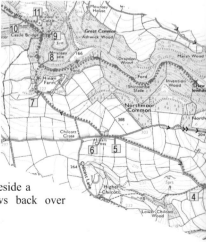

Forking left up an old sunken path for 'Beech Tree' it's a steep climb through the woods. Picking our way over a rocky section and zigzagging up to a field gate, we keep right beside a hedge to a crest with fine views back over **Dulverton**.

Crossing a farm track beside a large barn (Wp.3 18M) we go straight across a sloping field overlooking a pretty wooded valley; then it's over a stile and on beside a hedge before swinging right to another stile next to a stone cottage (for the shorter walk go down the right hand track).

Turning right onto a lane (Wp.4 26M) and climbing steadily uphill along the National Park boundary, we have

Overlooking the wooded valley

glimpses to our left of rolling hills and pastures; as the gradient eases we stroll beside tall beech hedges to **Hinam Cross** (Wp.5 41M) bearing left for 'East Anstey'.

After two minutes, going right into a 'No through road' (Wp.6 43M), we descend into the **Barle Valley** to a track junction; in autumn herds of red deer may be seen grazing in the fields on our right. Bearing left onto a woodland track (Wp.7 54M) then immediately right on a rough stony surface, we keep left downhill at a track fork, dropping to cross a stream before reaching the riverbank (Wp.8 60M).

Going left along a broad beech covered trail we stroll to **Castle Bridge** at the confluence of **Dane's Brook** and the **Barle**, then follow the red tipped 'Hawkridge RUPP' (Wp.9 65M) up the side of the valley. After four minutes, when level with the ground on our right (Wp.10 69M), we turn sharp right onto a small unmarked path running back along the ridge to the ancient manmade fort of **Brewer's Castle** (Wp.11 71M). It's clear why this site was chosen by Iron Age settlers as a defensive position as it stands on a narrow neck of land high above two river valleys; today woodland covers the slopes obscuring a 360 degree view, however, it is a delightful secluded picnic spot.

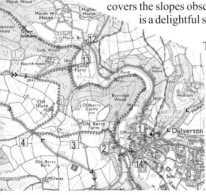

The earthworks resemble circular tiers of a wedding cake; just past its summit we swing right downhill (SE) over several levels; initially indistinct, the path soon becomes obvious, descending steeply to **Castle Bridge**. To explore the larger fort of **Mounsey Castle** on the opposite bank of the **Barle**, turn left for 100 yards upstream and over an unusual slatted wood footbridge.

Castle Bridge

Our return route to 'Dulverton' re-crosses **Castle Bridge**, and with the river on our left we pick up the 'Footpath to Marsh Bridge' (78M), climbing above the river to bear left along a broad well-trodden track; for the next half an hour this book can be put away as we wind along the deep valley on a clear undulating track crossing several rivulets.

It's a quiet woodland walk, mainly through mature broad-leaved trees mixed with occasional stands of conifers; herons, dippers and other water-loving birds may be seen beside the river.

Reaching a road (Wp.12 116M), a yellow-tipped 'Dulverton' sign points us right for 250 yards, then left through a kissing gate (Wp.13 119M) on a footpath between the buildings. Following the path across a stream, we bear left along the edge of a wood to the riverbank.

After climbing to a bench we drop back down to the bank before swinging away from the water along the foot of **Burridge Wood**, gradually gaining height until we reach 'Beech Tree' junction; framed by the trees **Dulverton** presents a pleasant picture. Continuing ahead, we return along the path and lane, turning left over the river bridge (Wp.14 145M) to the car park.

Dulverton, framed by trees

26 DULVERTON, MARSH BRIDGE & COURT DOWN

We suggest you allow half a day to enjoy this route along the **Barle Valley** and up to **Court Down's** pastures, taking time to amble around the market town of **Dulverton** and explore its historical attractions and eating places.

The statue of Lorna Doone standing next to **Exmoor House** marks the start of our walk; erected in 1854 as a Victorian Workhouse, the building now houses the **National Park Headquarters**. A pleasant valley path beside **Burridge Wood** brings us to **Marsh Bridge** and over an attractive packhorse bridge; after a steady climb through **Looseall Wood** up an ancient byway we enjoy widespread views from **Court Down** before returning to **Dulverton** through fields and along a track.

*Dulverton

Access by bus: First bus N°307 from **Barnstaple** and **Taunton**; First bus N°398 from **Tiverton** and **Minehead**.

| Extended walk |
| See Walk 25 |

Access by car: **Dulverton** is on the B 3222, 2 miles off the A396 connecting **Tiverton** (13 miles) and **Minehead** (19 miles). It is 10 miles from **Exford** on the B3223. Car parks are in the town centre and by the river.

| Stroll |
| From Wp.1 follow route towards **Marsh Bridge** and return the same way. |

From the riverside car park we cross **Barle** bridge (Wp.1 0M), turning immediately right up a lane, then bearing right on a public footpath between mossy banks. We fork right for 'Tarr Steps and Hawkridge' (Wp.2 4M), our broad path gently descending through trees with views over river and town. Our route runs along the foot of **Burridge Woods** beside a meadow, curving left to the river bank.

Beside the River Barle

After strolling beneath a beech canopy we tackle a short ascent and descent before sweeping away from the river beside a *layered hedgerow*. Keeping right around the base of a hill following a yellow tipped 'Marsh Bridge' sign (Wp.3 23M), we cross a stream onto a track heading towards **Kennel Farm**; there are good views of the steeply wooded **Barle Valley**. Going between outbuildings to a kissing gate we turn right down a lane, continuing straight on past a 'Tarr Steps' sign (Wp.4 29M), and over the white metal structure of **Marsh Bridge.** Just beyond, in a delightful riverside setting, we cross a tiny packhorse bridge to go ahead up a short length of road to a junction with the B3223, carefully cutting across a sharp bend into a red signed R.U.P.P. to 'Court Down and Northcombe' (Wp.5 31M).

Now we steadily crunch our way up through woods on an old sunken track edged with a mossy stone faced bank; originally constructed with thousands upon thousands of small stones, much has now crumbled away but the quality of craftsmanship can still be appreciated.

... fine views up the Barle Valley ...

Near the hilltop, bearing left out of the wood at a track T-junction, we follow a 'Winsford' sign through a gate, turning immediately right beside a hedge bank for 'Court Down' (Wp.6 49M). Keeping a few yards out from the bank, we skirt a pit and climb a field towards the brow of the hill; there are fine views back up the **Barle Valley** as we go through a right hand pedestrian gate, then diagonally right across a pasture to a Trig Point on **Court Down** (Wp.7 56M 316 metres).

Surrounded by fields and pastures, the excellent hilltop panorama includes **Haddon Hill**, **Dunkery Beacon** and **Dartmoor** in the far distance. Turning sharp right downhill (SW) and aiming for a pair of gates in the hedge, we go through the left gate on a blue-tipped 'Bridleway to Dulverton', strolling beside a right hand hedge with views stretching down to **Dulverton** and the valley beyond.

Going straight on beneath a stand of trees and through two more gates (Wp.8 64M), we follow a 'Bridleway' sign down a small sunken path, then slightly right through a large gap in a hedge. Now with a fence on our left, our route passes under a huge beech tree, just beyond which, beside a signpost pointing back to 'Court Down', we turn sharp right through a metal gate onto a R.U.P.P. (Wp.9 69M). We turn left towards 'Dulverton' our stony track runs down a ridge with occasional views into a steeply wooded valley on our left; arriving above the rooftops of **Dulverton**, we bend left on a tarmac lane to the end of a church wall (Wp.10 81M).

Bearing right down a path past a cobbled lane of attractive cottages we take the second gate on our right into **All Saint's** churchyard; although the tower is 13th century, the remainder of the substantial building is Victorian. Leaving the churchyard under a lych-gate, we amble down into the wide **Fore Street** past the **Lion Hotel** and **Town Hall** to the **Exmoor National Park Information Centre** (Wp.11 86M); for the riverside car park we turn right along a path, passing the **Guildhall Heritage Centre**, then over a *leat* to our start (Wp.12 88M). For refreshments there are several inns and tearooms to choose from; **Lewis's Tearooms** is a favourite of ours - no tea bags here and a strainer is provided!

27 WITHYPOOL, TARR STEPS & PORCHESTER'S POST

The winding path running downstream from **Withypool** through the woods and river meadows of the **Barle Valley** is a splendid route to one of Exmoor's most visited attractions; the famous and much photographed *clapper bridge* at **Tarr Steps**. Our return route climbs a bridleway onto remote open moorland with a panoramic display of both Exmoor and **Dartmoor**, to a stone circle on **Withypool Common**; although not as impressive as the *clapper bridge* it is the largest Exmoor has to offer.

Apart from a steep slog out of the valley after **Tarr Steps** the terrain offers comfortable walking, mainly on well defined tracks and paths; a short unmarked moorland section requires careful navigation, but if the weather is foggy an alternative route is available through lanes to **Withypool**.

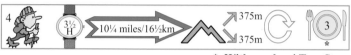

| 4 | 3½ H | 10¼ miles/16½km | 375m / 375m | ↻ | 3 * |

* **Withypool** and **Tarr Steps**

<table>
<tr><td>Shorter route
(7¾ miles/12.5km, ascents & descents 290metres) From Wp.8, continue down path to lane and turn right to Withypool.</td><td>Access by car: Turn off the B3223 at Comer Cross, half way between Dulverton and Simonsbath. Withypool car park is 1 mile downhill beside the river (SS 845354)</td></tr>
</table>

River Barle between Wps. 3&4

We go left along the lane from **Withypool** car park (Wp.1 0M), over the river bridge and past the Post Office and the old Shell petrol pumps, climbing the hill out of this quiet pretty village to 'Tarr Steps' permitted path. Crossing the stile on our right (Wp.2 9M) we bear left along a yellow-marked path dropping into the broad **Barle Valley** with lovely views upstream to **Landacre**; we go over a stile and through a gate onto the river bank. Entering a meadow we soon pass a set of stepping stones (Wp.3 18M); from here to **Tarr Steps** the waymarks alternate between blue and yellow, however, the river is always on our right.

Strolling downstream on a well trodden grass bridleway we stay beside or just above the river; this is

Looking back on Tarr Steps

comfortable walking through occasional gates and stiles, across big meadows and beneath overhanging beeches, their leaves changing with the seasons from bright lime to dark green and bronze.

Treading through a springtime carpet of bluebells to the end of the public bridleway we continue at the signpost on an established permitted path (Wp.4 50M). Our route through the trees becomes stony and twisty for a while before we emerge between steep open slopes to pass a private river footbridge.
From here, an increasing number of casual walkers herald our approach to **Tarr Steps**.

Going straight on over a footbridge by a bridleway sign (Wp.5 73M), we nimbly make our way along an uneven flagstone pavement beside the river's edge; forking right after 9 minutes down a 'Footpath' into a river meadow leading to **Tarr Steps** (Wp.6 86M).

This is a year round tourist honeypot; the size and length of the *clapper bridge* make it unique on Exmoor, arguments continue whether it is a medieval construction or earlier, but it leaves a strong visual impression as we turn right across the large slabs onto a lane.

Bearing right after 30 yards up the fern lined 'Hawkridge' bridleway, this steep slog is a rude awakening, especially if you've just eaten lunch! As we swing right through a gate beside a mossy stone wall there are views across the valley to **Winsford Hill**. Turning left in front of the next field gate and still climbing (W) through another gate, the gradient eases as we follow the hedge over the crest and dip slightly to a gate at **Parsonage Farm** (Wp.7 104M). Going right on the 'Withypool Hill' track, we gently climb through fields and gates to the brow, enjoying panoramic views of the moorland tops beyond **Withypool.**

Starting our descent, we cross a stile onto a path (here the shorter route to **Withypool** goes straight on) and immediately on our left is an unsigned metal field gate with a distinctive rectangular pattern (Wp.8 113M). Turning left, we head straight up hill (WSW) away from the left hedge; as the gradient lessens we bear gently right to a gate in the middle of the far hedge, continuing straight on beside the field boundary to come out onto a lane (Wp.9 123M).

Crossing over, we join a yellow-marked permitted footpath to 'Withypool and Porchester's Post', walking beside the left hedge across two fields and through a gate onto the moor where a narrow path towards **Old Barrow** lies straight ahead (W). A low cairn 200 yards in front marks the plateau top (Wp.10 131M), giving us tremendous views, from **Dartmoor** on our left around to **Dunkery Beacon**.

There is no defined path ahead as we aim (WNW) for the far end of the belt of trees running along our right; clumping through the tussock grass past a small wire enclosure, we gradually bear right to go through a gap between the tree belt and a bank ahead. Now climbing a well defined track (NNW) to a gate in the far hedge, (Wp.11 145M) we continue in the same direction to another gate, bearing left (NW) parallel with the field boundary to a broad track.

Just through the gate on our left stands a 12 foot wooden obelisk named **Porchester's Post** (Wp.12 157M); an inscription gives the reasons for it's re-erection in 2002. Going back through the gate striding down a dirt track towards **Withypool** we pass the splendidly named **Tudball's Splats,** an old animal enclosure; our track gently climbs a small crest to a path crossroads (Wp.13 167M, if you don't wish to visit the stone circle, continue ahead to Wp.16).

Tudball's Splats & Withypool Hill

Bearing diagonally right (ENE), we climb a narrow path over heather clad **Withypool Common** into a clearing, to stumble upon the remnants of Exmoor's largest stone circle (Wp.14 177M). Although little is known about the symbolic meaning of these ancient ruins perhaps a more modern explanation can be found; for aficionados of The Hitch Hikers Guide to the Galaxy the number of paces across the circle's diameter is 42!

Continuing in the same direction, a short climb brings us to the top of **Withypool Hill**; (Wp.15 181M 398 metres) after admiring the far reaching views, we turn left down a path to a track junction (Wp.16 190M), then right along a broad track to the roadside.

Curving right along the 'Withypool contour track' above the white cottages dotted in the valley, we start our gradual descent before bearing left after 15 minutes towards the last of the hillside houses, for a final steep descent along the village lane (Wp.17 213M).

28 HADDON HILL, HADDEO VALLEY & WIMBLEBALL LAKE

Unique on Exmoor this large lake with its sweeping panorama is the main feature of this varied walk. **Wimbleball Lake** lies on the softer south east boundary of the National Park surrounded by heath land, attractive hamlets and a tranquil river valley.

Haddon Hill with uplifting views across **Wimbleball Lake** is set in the rolling Somerset countryside. Our route runs down an ancient sunken track to the timeless hamlet of **Bury** followed by a relaxing riverside stroll along an 18th century carriage drive in the wonderful setting of the **Haddeo Valley**. A short stiff climb brings us to the reservoir and a splendid lakeside walk includes crossing the dam, returning up the heath covered slopes of **Haddon Hill** and with luck catching sight of sturdy Exmoor ponies.

3	3H	8¾ miles/14km	290m / 290m	↻	1*

* at **Wimbleball Reservoir Tea-room** and Shop (seasonal)

Access by car: 5 miles from **Bampton** along B3190. **Haddon Hill** car park (SS 969285) is on the left at the top of the hill. From the **Watchet** direction the car park is on the right 1½ miles after the village of **Upton**.

> **Shorter route**
> Walk up the service road from Wp.7 to the car park (6¼ miles/10km)

Wimbleball Lake from Haddon Hill

From the **Haddon Hill** information board (Wp.1 0M) we stroll left along the length of the car park to the five barred gate at the right side of the line of trees, heading steadily up onto heath land along the main track (W) towards the trig point with views of **Wimbleball Lake** below.

Much of the area on our left was covered with conifers until 2004 when the timber was felled returning the land to lowland heath. Designated a European Special Area of Conservation, protected endangered species include a colony of heath fritillary butterflies. The Exmoor National Park team actively manage the heath; however, day to day operations are delegated to specialists - a herd of Exmoor ponies grazing the slopes, contentedly munching their way through a key dietary ingredient, gorse!

After half a mile our track crests the hill passing the trig point on our left dropping gently down with distant views and glimpses into the steep wooded **Haddeo valley**. Our route flattens and narrows as we fork left (Wp.2 13M) on a path which veers left (S) across a path junction, before descending past a

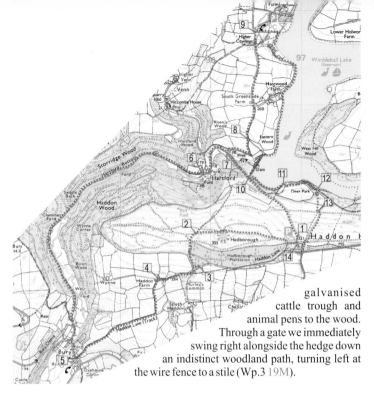

galvanised cattle trough and animal pens to the wood. Through a gate we immediately swing right alongside the hedge down an indistinct woodland path, turning left at the wire fence to a stile (Wp.3 19M).

Over the stile we turn right along a dirt track passing the farm buildings to bear left, just before the barns, and go through the gate (Wp.4 24M) down the 'Bridleway' into sunken Haddon Lane. This is an ancient country track where millions of footsteps and hooves have eroded the surface so much that the earth banks now stretch high above our heads sprouting unkempt gnarled trees.

Haddon Lane (after Wp.4)

Mainly uneven bedrock, this slippery track doubles up as a stream during wet weather; we can't get lost, just follow the track through the gates down hill. Part way, after swinging right, the track follows a ridge with pleasant views into the valleys, then its back to bedrock carefully picking our way to a road junction at the pretty hamlet of **Bury** tucked down in the valley floor (Wp.5 43M).

We turn right past the chapel along the lane either fording the river or crossing the old cobbled bridge (see picture over page) towards the church and school. These are now converted into dwellings but outwardly at least the hamlet loses none of its rustic charm.

The cobbled bridge at Bury

Bearing right along a lane and track to **Bury Lodge**, we go through the gate joining the 'Bridleway to Hartford'. The Lodge marks the start of **Lady Harriet Acland Drive**, part of an old network of local estate tracks.

In the heyday of horse drawn carriages these often used tracks were well maintained, topped with a layer of cream coloured chippings; the main roads of their time! Today the track has many potholes but it is easier walking than Haddon Lane and we can appreciate the peace and quiet of the **Haddeo Valley** as it was a century ago; no need now for the guide book until **Hartford**.

It is easy to be startled by one of Exmoor's scariest sounds; the sudden flapping and strident squawking of a disturbed pheasant as it lumbers skywards from one of the many pheasantrys. There are various names for families of pheasants, e.g. a nide or nye, our favourite is a bouquet of pheasants; an apt expression for such a colourful bird.

Strolling upriver beside pastures set between tree-covered slopes we eventually pass **Exmoor Fisheries** and **Hartford Lodge** to arrive at the hamlet of **Hartford,** forking right to the gate and 'Hartford Mill' sign (Wp.6 86M). Going through the gate along the bridleway, we turn left along the river bank on the 'public footpath' crossing a footbridge then left again on the grassy bridleway curving round the base of the hill to join a concrete road for 'Upton'. Passing the cattle grid beside the river with its moss covered stones we arrive at a junction where the service road continues up the hill (Wp.7 94M); for the shorter walk go up this road past the dam to the car park.

Our route goes left on the 'Permitted footpath', over the river footbridge and along the path for 100 yards to a path junction. We go through the gate and right along a sunken bridleway towards the towering structure of the dam which looms into view supported by enormous grey buttresses; virtually the same height as Nelson's Column. Fortunately, before we disappear into the bowels of the dam our path goes sharply left and we slog up the steep hill to join a concrete track (Wp.8 104M) where the full expanse of the retaining wall can be appreciated; still climbing, we pass a cattle grid and farm buildings bearing left at a road junction to the brow of the hill.

After our climb we relax with a short stroll along the lane past the Wimbleball Sailing Club entrance, then a house, turning right into the main entrance for **Wimbleball Reservoir** (Wp.9 119M). There are plenty of picnic tables to enjoy a break in this splendid location and during the season a tearoom and gift shop is open. The lake is well used by anglers, sailors and windsurfers; the camp site overlooks the water and footpaths provide a range of easy routes around the reservoir.

Continuing straight ahead towards the lake beside the right hand hedge our path passes the children's 'Play Area'. At a 'Lakeside Walk, Dam 1 mile' signpost we turn right round the side and back of the Sailing Club keeping the lake on our left. Our easy lakeside route continues along a grassy path entering a wooded area before swinging right to arrive at the top of the Dam.

Wimbleball Lake

The reservoir was completed in 1979 and is the only major lake in the National Park. Its concrete buttress dam holds 21,320 mega litres of water, with a surface area of 150 hectares and mainly supplies Exeter and East Devon. The lake is used for many recreational activities. Information about easy access short walks is available from the **Wimbleball** reservoir shop.

Crossing the Dam to the far end of the parapet we turn immediately left on a small footpath 'Upton 2, path suitable for summer use only' (Wp.10 146M); you can use it all year round, walking through the trees to cross a stile beside the path (Wp.11 152M). Stepping a few paces into the old deer park we bear left along the track through the 'Haddon Hill' gate to a path junction (Wp.12 158M); the 'Footpath to Car Park' sign directs us right uphill (S) through gorse bushes and light trees to a track T-junction (Wp.13 162M).

We turn left for 10 yards and then right up a narrow path for a few paces to the woodland edge, swinging immediately right up the hill beside the trees (SSW). Our indistinct path becomes clearer as it wends up through the gorse and heather to a track T-junction where we turn right to join the road, then left into a copse. Just before the locked road gate, we bear right to the fence and through a gate to return to the car park and a final view of the lake (Wp.14 172M).

This stunning linear route captures the essence of Exmoor's wooded valleys, following the course of the **East Lyn** river valley from **County Gate** to **Lynmouth**. Starting on open slopes high above the **Bristol Channel** we drop into the valley at **Brendon** where a riverside track winds between trees to **Rockford**, continuing through mature woods to lovely **Watersmeet**.

A stiff climb takes us past an Iron Age settlement onto the lofty heights of **Myrtleberry Cleave** for a stroll above the tree line to **Summer House Hill**; greeted by impressive views over **Lynton** and the cliffs to **Foreland Point**, we finally descend steeply through woods to **Lynmouth**.

The bus ride from **Lynmouth** over **Countisbury Hill** along part of 'Britain's prettiest bus journey' is a terrific way to reach our start point; for fine coastal views, sit on the side opposite the bus driver. The route although hilly, is along clear paths and tracks; note that GPS reception is unreliable on the valley floor between waypoints 4&5 and after Wp.9 to **Lynmouth**.

3/4   2¾ H   7.4 miles/11.9km   350m / 650m   *   4 **

* first ½ mile of route above **Ashton Cleave**
** **Rockford, Brendon, Watersmeet, Lynton & Lynmouth**

Less hilly valley walk
From **Rockford** continue along the river path to **Watersmeet** and **Lynmouth** (7 miles/11.3km ascents 150 metres, descents 450 metres).

Stroll
From **County Gate** take the signed footpath to the remains of the Roman Fortlet on **Old Burrow Hill** (2½ miles).

Access by bus: N°300 bus Ilfracombe-Minehead - from Lyndale Bridge, Lynmouth

Access by car: Park at **Lynmouth**

The superb panorama from **County Gate** can best be appreciated from the far end of the car park (Wp.1 0M) using the engraved metal sketch which identifies the visible topographical features.

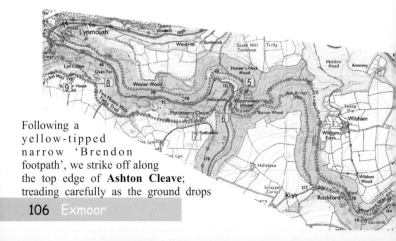

Following a yellow-tipped narrow 'Brendon footpath', we strike off along the top edge of **Ashton Cleave**; treading carefully as the ground drops

steeply away to our left and pausing to admire the views.

Descending beside a field edge, a signpost (Wp.2 11M) points us through a gate for 'Brendon'; crossing rough pasture, we swing around a small valley and turn right over a footbridge and stile. Our route now crosses a field to a boundary ahead where wooden steps lead onto a bracken covered slope; going along a path through a gate, we climb up the valley side to the brow.

As we descend, the houses of **Brendon** are visible nestling in the valley below; we wind round a gully and head up to a pedestrian gate on the skyline. Descending through heather and bracken into a field, we turn sharp left along its edge, then bear right down to a lane and left around a bend

Looking towards Brendon

to a road junction (Wp.3 40M). Continuing straight on past two bridges on our left, we bear left on a track at a 'Rockford' sign (Wp.4 44M), going through a gate marked 'Countisbury Mill'.

The cobbled causeway

Heading to a gate marked 'Footpath only', we go between stone buildings along a grass path by the appropriately named **Peace Cottage**, to the **East Lyn** river bank. Unexpectedly encountering a short section of cobbled causeway, we join a broad comfortable path for a relaxing woodland stroll beside the river; regularly placed benches indicate **National Trust** land. The river rushes through rocky cuttings, tumbling over boulders to a footbridge at **Rockford** (66M); a less hilly riverside path for 'Watersmeet and Lynmouth' goes straight on. However, we cross the river, turning right for refreshments (including Rockford real ale) at **The Rockford Inn**. Continuing along the lane, we climb past cottages and turn right through a gate (73M) onto a 'Watersmeet' bridleway. Heading down a woodland track, we fork left and climb gently beside moss covered outcrops, before starting our gradual descent to **Watersmeet.**

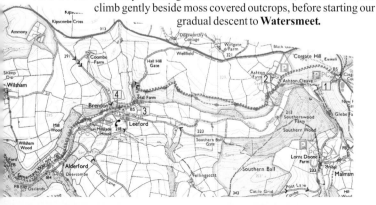

Bearing left at a bridleway T-junction (89M), we enjoy glimpses across the valley through sun-dappled glades and springtime bluebells, forking right just above the riverbank on a 'Watersmeet' path (95M). To our right **Watersmeet House** stands in a beautiful location; once a hunting and fishing lodge, it is now operated by the **National Trust** as a seasonal tea room and information point.

Views to South Hill Common (Wp.6)

Bending left to cross a footbridge over **Hoaroak Water**, we ascend to a path marked 'Lynton over the Cleaves' (99M), bearing right to cross a road (Wp.5 102M). Our path climbs steeply, swinging left across **Myrtleberry North Iron Age Enclosure** to the foot of a long flight of steps (Wp.6 111M); time for a break to take in the views to **South Hill Common**.

Now, tackling the steps, we pause at a strategically placed halfway bench, before sinking gratefully onto the top one; for those not wishing to count from step 1 - the answer is 134! The reward for our strenuous effort is a splendid view along the length of the valley and on a clear day the **Brecon Beacons** can be seen over 20 miles away across the **Bristol Channel**.

Gradually climbing to a signpost and bearing right for 'Lynmouth' (Wp.7 118M), our path levels out above the tree line; after going through a pair of gates and past a stone seat, we descend around hairpin bends to a tiny bridge across a stream. Now, regaining our lost height by zigzagging back up, a final turn past a bench brings us up a gentler gradient to the hill top, with views to **Countisbury Church** and **Butter Hill**.

Foreland Point

Going straight on and ignoring signs to 'West Lyn' on our left and 'Lynmouth' on our right (Wp.8 144M), we continue along the hillside towards 'Lynbridge' for 3 minutes. At the next path junction (Wp.9 147M), our route to **Lynmouth** bends sharply right downhill; however, it is worth going on for a few paces to get the best views of **Lynton, Lynmouth** and coastal views along red sandstone cliffs to **Foreland Point**.

Retracing our steps we descend a steep woodland path, following several 'Public footpath signs to Lynmouth', eventually entering a small walled path, then a tarmac alleyway.

After winding steeply down between cottages we emerge onto a road opposite a church, turning left to **Lyndale Bridge** car park (165M).

30 CHERITON, HOAROAK WATER, EXE HEAD & PINKERY POND

The high ground south of **Lynton** offers a real sense of exploration and exhilarating walking over remote moorland, coupled with terrific views and historic connections. Until the mid 19th century much of this part of central Exmoor could only be covered on foot or horseback using ancient trackways and our route runs along sections of these ridgeway's and packhorse trails.

From **Combe Park Wood** we climb steeply onto **Cheriton Ridge**, heading across the moor to **Hoar Oak Tree**, a boundary marker of the **Exmoor Royal Forest**. Striding along the upper reaches of **Hoaroak Water** through a bare narrow valley, our ascent to **Exe Head** is followed by level moorland walking via **Pinkery Pond**, **Woodbarrow Gate** and **Shallowford**. Our final section through pastures is a complete contrast, before we descend along a woodland path into the delightful **Hoaroak** river valley.

A GPS or compass is essential for the moorland sections, particularly in poor weather.

4/5   4½ H   13½ miles/22km   500m / 500m   0

Access by car: **Combe Park Wood** National Trust car park (SS 740477) is located 3 miles south of **Lynmouth** at **Hillsford Bridge**; the junction of the A39 and B3223.

Shorter walk
To **Hoar Oak** Wp.7, return across **Furzehill Common** to Wp.16. (8½ miles/13.7km, ascents/descents 300 metres) See directions at end of main walk description.

Stroll
Along **Hoaroak Water** to **Smallcombe Bridge** and return. (1½ miles/2.4 km)

From the car park (Wp.1 0M) our route follows the 'Cheriton' signs climbing out of the trees and across a field before we turn left on an enclosed path behind the high walls of **Combe Park House** to a pedestrian gate (Wp.2 7M). Forking left on the 'Riverside Walk' along a pleasant bridleway beside **Hoaroak Water**, we cross **Smallcombe Bridge** (Wp.3 15M) to be faced with a stiff climb up the rough track past **Scoresdown Farm** before the gradient eases. Turning right at the second track junction (Wp.4 25M), we head between grass banks for 'Cheriton Ridge and Exe Head' through a gate onto the moor. Moving away from the left hand wall, following the 'MW' sign, we gently ascend the middle of the broad **Cheriton Ridge** (SSE) heading for the high point; there isn't a clear track to start with, but this is easy terrain and some 4x4 vehicle ruts head in the right direction.

At the summit our efforts are rewarded with glorious 360 degree moorland views (Wp.5 43M 359 metres); looking ahead just to our right, we can see our next destination, the entrance to a narrow valley with a circular sheepfold on the adjacent slope. This is great moorland walking as we take the broad right hand track striding down the ridge, parallel to the valley on our right, before curving down to a junction near the river (Wp.6 63M). Ignoring the right hand rutted track, we continue on a path along the bank of **Hoaroak Water**, avoiding any boggy patches by taking higher ground along the base of the hill, to arrive at a gate in the **Exmoor Forest** wall (Wp.7 71M). The **Hoar Oak**, protected by a wooden fence, is the latest in a series of oaks to be planted over hundreds of years in this exposed spot marking the Forest boundary with **Lynton** and **Brendon** Commons.

Going right, across **Hoaroak Water** to a path junction, we turn left for 'Exe Head' on a level man-made path wending its way along a bare narrow valley above a dwindling stream.

... a level man-made path ...

For the short walk, turn right and follow the directions at end of main walk description. In August 1952 following a torrential downpour this area became a water-logged sponge, releasing vast quantities of water, which together with other swollen rivers became a deadly deluge that flooded **Lynmouth**.

Curving beneath a rocky outcrop and a ruined sheepfold, we ford the stream by **Long Chains Combe**, climbing steadily up a stony track onto the moor at **Exe Head** (Wp.8 97M), the watershed between north and east Devon rivers.

We head right along a track towards 'Pinkery Pond' and continue through a gate into rough pasture, following blue paint marks beside a right hand fence. On this stretch the level ground can be heavy underfoot, as we weave around the soggier bits to a gate and on to a sign for 'Chains Barrow' (Wp.9 124M); here we can take a short detour to the trig point (487 metres) erected on top of a *tumulus*. Our route continues beside the right hand fence through a landscape of flat featureless moorland tussocks

contrasting with verdant valley floors and smooth hills rolling towards the coast. Where a field wall blocks our way ahead, we swing right then left through a gate, before dropping to **Pinkery Pond** (Wp.10 137M); this small reservoir was built by **John Knight** in the 19th century, possibly as part of an ambitious but unsuccessful project to supply water power for a mineral railway near **Simonsbath**.

Continuing across the earth dam (0M) by the fence and climbing to a corner gate, we follow the path slightly right (NW) to **Woodbarrow Gate** (Wp.11 11M); this track junction marks the intersection of the east west ridgeway we have just walked with an ancient north south packhorse trail.

Turning right, we follow the 'Barbrook' bridleway diagonally left for 2 minutes along the side of a low mound that marks the trail (NNW); as a steep ravine appears on our left, the track swings gently right in a northerly direction across flat open moor. Picking our way carefully across the plateau, avoiding some wet sections, we head (N) towards expansive views of the coast and **Bristol Channel**.

Approaching Wp.12

We skirt the corner of a big earth bank and go through a gate by a row of trees (Wp.12 26M), steadily descending a track along the margins of the moor before turning right onto a common at **Shallowford Farm** (Wp.13 44M).

Crossing a stream, we curve right onto **Ilkerton Ridge** to a track roundabout, taking the second track from the right heading (ESE) over the crest; as **North Furzehill** hamlet appears on our left we bear towards it, aiming for the grey roofed white house tucked in at the edge of the common. Going through a gate on our left, we wend our way along a track, passing a waterwheel, to emerge onto a lane by a cattle grid (Wp.14 63M). Turning sharp left into **North Furzehill Farm** then immediately right, we drop into a lovely little dell complete with its own miniature **Tarr Steps**. Taking the middle field gate and keeping right over a stile we follow the hedge, continuing in the same direction (NNW) across pastures, negotiating several gates and stiles, including a rare Exmoor ladder stile, to go left onto a lane.

We keep right by the farm house on a short valley track, then turn left over a tiny stream to go up through a gate and onto a lane (Wp.15 82M). Here we bear right to **Sparhanger Cross**, then right again, before joining a stony 'Cheriton Bridleway', to go left at a path crossroad (Wp.16 93M) for 'Lyndown'.

The sculpted hedges

Strolling (N) through four level fields beside hedgebanks, first on our left, then on our right, we can enjoy far reaching views and admire the beech hedges growing from the bank tops, sculpted into 45 degree shapes by the prevailing westerly winds.

As we round the top of a *combe*, a gate opens onto a brief length of track leading to a recycling point (Wp.17 109M); turning right downhill for 5 minutes, we leave the lane through a left hand gate on the 'Woodland walk to Combe Park' path. Now strolling through mature woodland above **Hoaroak Water** and ignoring a 'Watersmeet' sign, we reach the 'Riverside Walk' junction, to return left past **Combe Park House** to the car park (Wp.18 131M).

Shorter route
From the signpost (Wp.A1) we go right for 'Furze Hill and Stock Common' following the track down to a metal gate; then climb past a derelict building on a blue marked track to a field corner. Heading (NW) on to the moor the path gradually peters out as we head along the top of the ridge to a gate (Wp.A2) in the fence ahead. Although there's no path our route goes straight ahead (NNW) over a slight rise, beyond which we follow the left hand stone wall to a gate (Wp.A3). Following the 'Footpath' signs through three fields to a gate (Wp.A4), we enter a delightful grass track for 'Sparhanger and Cheriton' strolling to a track T-junction (Wp.A5), turning left along a muddy tree canopied track to Wp.16.

31 EXFORD, LARKBARROW & TROUT HILL

During this grand walk we uncover some of Exmoor's industrial past when strenuous efforts were made to extract minerals; hard to believe today, but railways and canals were part of a plan to utilise this area's natural resources.

From **Exford**, strolling along pleasant country lanes and tracks we climb to **Larkbarrow Corner**, then out onto rolling moors, following the bed of an uncompleted railway into the higher reaches of the beautiful **Exe Valley**. A short stiff climb up a remote hillside onto **Trout Hill** gives a fine panorama and a feeling of being on top of the world as we head down to **Badgworthy Water**. Our return along easy tracks passes **Larkbarrow**'s ruined farm and crosses **Almsworthy Common** before a final bridleway descent into **Exford**. This long route can be significantly shortened by walking the moorland section only between **Larkbarrow Corner** and **Alderman's Barrow**. A GPS or compass is essential across the moor, particularly in poor weather; this is preferably a walk for fine days.

5	5¼ H	15 miles/24km		455m / 455m		3

Access by bus: First bus N°398 limited service from **Tiverton** and **Dulverton**

Access by car: **Exford** is on the B3224, 5 miles west of **Wheddon Cross**. From **Dulverton** and **Lynmouth** take the B3223. The car park is in the village (SS 854384).

Shorter moorland walk
Start from **Larkbarrow Corner** (SS 824415): 8¾ miles/14km, ascents & descents 230 metres. Park in the nearby lay-by and walk from Wp.5 to Wp.16, returning down the lane.

Turning left from the car park, (Wp1 0M), we stroll past the ivy clad **White Horse Inn** and over the **River Exe** to bear right along the road, then right for 'Edgcott' up a wooden staircase. Walking along a field edge over two stiles, we re-cross the river heading through a meadow to the right hand hedge, stepping over a plank and stile into **Edgcott Road** (WP2 12M). Turning left and then keeping left at a fork, our pleasant lane winds between pretty cottages up a quiet valley; soon after **Dunscombe Farm** we turn right up a narrow lane at a 'Larkbarrow Bridleway' signpost towards **Hill Farm** (Wp3 27M).

After a steep 5 minute ascent between beech topped banks the lane turns left; we go straight on through a gate, climbing a track to a ridge top; with valley views on either side, our well used gated track runs beside hedgerows, reaching a lane between two round stone pointed pillars (Wp4 49M). Turning right, we gradually climb to **Larkbarrow Corner** (64M), going through a left hand gate (Wp5 0M) on the 'Simonsbath' bridleway.

Simonsbath bridle way

After 175 yards we go through another gate keeping beside the right hand bank for a few paces towards a 'Bridleway' sign; **five yards before the sign** our route bears left (Wp.6 3M) heading across the moor (WSW).

Our path runs either along or beside a slight mound, gradually curving right before resuming its direction (WSW). This 19th century railway bed was designed to carry iron ore to **Porlock** for shipment to **Wales**; the rails were never laid but the contour route, although sometimes a bit bumpy, is good walking.

The gate at Wp.8

To our left looking down **Sparcombe Water** there are wonderful views of the upper **Exe Valley** and *cleave*. After passing a field corner (Wp.7 25M) at the head of **Rams Combe** we continue beside a left hand bank to adjacent gates; the field gate has 3 closing hooks plus a latch, so the pedestrian gate is easier (Wp.8 38M); exactly at longitude SS 80000.

Now striding along a blue marked track downhill through a gate, we bear left at **Warren Farm**'s beech trees and keep left onto a tarmac lane, dropping to a gate just before a river bridge (Wp.9 50M). We turn right (not signed), up a track for 80 yards to the point at which it curves right; finding a narrow path straight on between the bracken, we pick our way along the hillside to a gate above the river. Continuing along the open slope for 150 yards towards a large snout-shaped rock formation; we bear right in front of it, scrambling up the side of a gully (NW) on a narrow path that peters out above the rocks where there are beautiful views to **Prayway Head** (see photo over page). Bearing diagonally right uphill NNW, we slog over grass clumps, reeds and an old

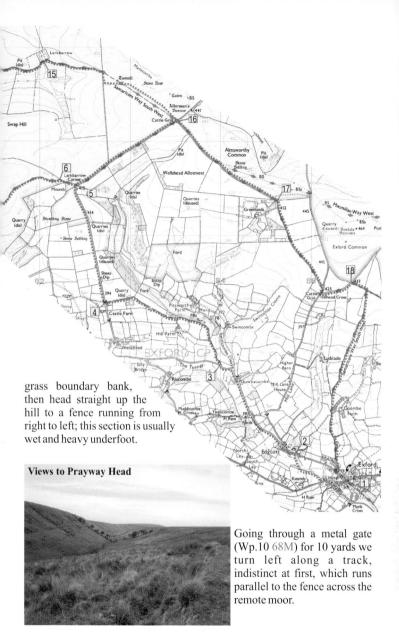

grass boundary bank, then head straight up the hill to a fence running from right to left; this section is usually wet and heavy underfoot.

Views to Prayway Head

Going through a metal gate (Wp.10 68M) for 10 yards we turn left along a track, indistinct at first, which runs parallel to the fence across the remote moor.

Beside the fence is a small canal, now mainly filled with vegetation; this was dug as part of the railway project to provide water power for an incline plane near **Warren Farm.** Reaching a gate, we turn right in front of it (Wp.11 77M), walking beside the left hand fence heading north over the brow of **Trout Hill**; our reward for the uphill slog is a glorious moorland panorama down to the **Doone Valley** and over the **Bristol Channel** to **Wales**. In early summer we may be fortunate to see a herd of red deer hinds prancing up **Lanacombe**.

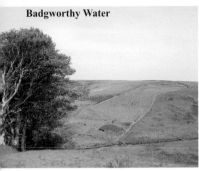
Badgworthy Water

When the fence starts to run along a substantial bank there is an easier path on the bank top; it's like walking along a miniature Hadrian's Wall, enjoying the moorland grandeur. Tramping down a gradual slope, the fence and wall eventually bend right by a clump of trees and with the fence bank on our left, we drop down a path through a tiny *combe* into the delightful setting of **Badgworthy Water** (Wp.12 113M).

Crossing over a footbridge we bear right, clambering a narrow path out of the valley; initially a goat track but at the top we curve right on a broad level grass path. We stay on high ground following the line of the stream below as it passes a footbridge, bends left, and meanders up to another bridge. Our path drops down towards the bridge but a few yards before reaching it (Wp.13 129M), we bear left, ascending a small valley with a stream on our right to a path junction beside a field boundary (Wp.14 136M). Going through a gate on a 'Larkbarrow and Exford' bridleway our track runs beside beech trees, gently climbing through gates and rough pastures to the bleak ruins of **Larkbarrow Farm** (Wp.15 154M); it was occupied until WWII when artillery practice blasted the buildings.

Stretching our legs on a well surfaced track we turn right at a 'Bridleway' sign, then left through a gate for 'Exford'. Heading east over heather, our rough path slowly swings (ESE) as we enjoy our last broad moorland views before climbing a stile onto a road (Wp.16 176M). To complete the shorter moorland walk we turn right down the lane to **Larkbarrow Corner** (192M).

Heading across the road (0M) onto a bridleway, we stride out over **Almsworthy Common,** following a hedge to the bottom of the hill, where we swing right through a gate (Wp.17 20M). Now strolling along a track between hedges we reach a T-junction, turning right into a lane and almost immediately left at **Hillhead Cross** for 'Stoke Pero'.

Leaving Almsworthy Common

At a **Porlock** road junction (Wp.18 38M), we turn right down a track for 'Exford and Stone Cross'; two minutes later a small sign points us right onto an 'Exford' bridleway. Wandering down a well marked route through fields, we lose the valley and moorland views back to **Dunkery Beacon** as our path becomes a sunken track, then a tarmac lane; at the T-junction with **Edgcott Road** we go left beside **Exford** village green to the car park (69M).

St. Mary's, Molland

Molland is part of a privately owned 6,800 acre estate on the south west moorland fringe of **Exmoor National Park**. The village church captures the timeless feeling of this walk; its light Georgian interior, virtually untouched since 1740 has heavy uneven flagstones, enclosed high backed pews and an impressive triple pulpit. After a 'fire and brimstone' sermon, carriages, carts and horses would have taken well-to-do churchgoers to Sunday lunch; for many, Shank's pony would have been their only means of transport and today for us it is still the best way to enjoy an unspoilt, imperceptibly changing landscape.

Leaving the village and going in and out of remote steep sided valleys to **Smallacombe**, we climb the smooth open slopes of **Molland Common** to **Anstey Gate**. We return via **Brimblecombe** and **Bremley Cross** through fields and woods along tiny country lanes and tracks. A GPS and compass are necessary in case of poor visibility across the common.

3 | 1H 55M | 5.3 miles/8.5km | 320m / 320m | ⟳ | 🍴 | 2*

* in **Molland**

Extended walk
Join with Walk 24 for a figure of eight route (11.1 miles/17.8km, ascents & descents 620 metres).

Access by car: Molland is 18 miles ESE from **Barnstaple**; A361, to **Haynes Cross**, left on B3227 and left at **Combesland Cross** following **Molland** signs. From **Dulverton** 9 miles W along ridge road over **West Anstey Common**. Park in lay-by in front of the Church (SS 808284).

Strolling from **St Mary's Church** (Wp.1 0M) to **The London Inn** and turning right up a tarmac track onto a 'Public Footpath' past **Church Farm,** we follow waymark signs diagonally right (ENE) over a field to a metal gate (Wp.2 5M). Gently climbing in the same direction across a second field to a lane, there are pleasant rural views to our right and back over **Molland**.

Crossing into a pasture, a footpath sign points us diagonally left towards the right hand end of a line of trees; going over the brow into a steep little *combe* we swing left down a broad grass path to the second 'Public Footpath'sign (Wp.3 11M). Going right over two footbridges and a stile we bear slightly left up the slope, climbing through a gate in a field corner, then beside the left hand hedge, before curving gently right onto a lane (Wp.4 17M).

Our route for 'Smallacombe' lies directly opposite along a tarmac lane; dropping between banks filled with summer flowers and ignoring a right hand bridleway we continue for 'Anstey Gate' beside the farm, taking the 'Bridleway' onto Access Land. We cross a concrete bridge, then splash through **Triss Combe** to curve left up a track to a path junction (Wp.5 22M); as the dirt track bends right, we bear slightly left up a grass path between gorse (NE) with **Smallacombe Combe** on our left.

Exmoor ponies

Leaving the rolling farmland behind, we gradually climb onto heather-clad **Molland Common**, ignoring paths on either side; if you're lucky and tread softly, you may spot red deer though more likely you'll encounter Exmoor ponies. Our path very gradually veers right as we aim ahead for the top left hand end of a line of trees at **Anstey Gate**.

At a multi-track junction (Wp.6 33M) we go straight on across **Gourt Mires** on a broad peaty track (ENE) gently ascending and swinging right (E), the ground not as bad as the term 'mires'might indicate. The track divides at the head of **Anstey's Combe** (Wp.7 43M), the steep valley cutting down to our right; forking left (E) the tree line comes back into view as we climb through heather to a cattle grid at **Anstey Gate** (Wp.8 54M). If you are ready for a break, there is a welcoming bench on the other side of the gate offering splendid views along the ridgeway and a panorama to **Dunkery Hill**, **Haddon Hill** and across Mid-**Devon** to **Dartmoor**.

Turning right (SSW), stepping over a wooden vehicle barrier, we head down a stony bridleway, gradually easing away from the left hand row of trees to arrive at a T-junction beside hedge boundaries; deep wooded valleys lie below us and beyond, a predominantly green variegated landscape rolls peacefully on across **Devon**. Bearing right for 150 yards beside the field edge to a 'Bremley Bridleway' (Wp.9 64M) we go left beside a black tin shed on a gravel farm track; after a pasture, our gated track winds left then right down the concrete surface of a sunken lane.

Going through double gates at the foot of the lane we turn right beside farm buildings (Wp.10 72M) into a blue-marked sunken track, very muddy after rain, heading straight on at a 'Bridleway' signpost (Wp.11 75M) into rough scrubby woodland seasoned with the pungent smell of wild garlic. Stepping over a little stream and through a gate we cross a footbridge into a small open valley; taking the right hand 'Bridleway' (Wp.12 77M) climbing steeply up through fir trees, a track joins from our right as we bear left on an easier

Woodland between Wps. 11&12

gradient broad track. Emerging onto the hilltop, big pastoral views suddenly open up; walking along the field edge our track drops between high hedges beside **Gourte Farm** and after crossing a cattle grid we bear left and climb up to **Bremley Cross** (Wp.13 94M) then down a ' Molland' lane past old mine workings.

Just over a stream, the lane bends left. On our right is a 'Public Bridleway' signpost (Wp.14 97M); on the same post a 'Public Footpath' sign points us up the bank on a short flight of steps and over a stile.

Climbing the steep slope after Wp.14

Climbing directly up a steep slope beside grassed over old mine workings we continue to a hedge beyond the top of a gully; going straight ahead over a stile and with more good views, it's level walking along field boundaries to a road at **Latchcombe Cross** (Wp.15 106M). (To avoid the steep field ascent continue along the lane from Wp.14 turning right to Wp.15).

Continuing straight on to **Molland** we dip in and out of a small valley, and after passing **Moor Lane Cross South** head for the church tower (Wp.16 115M); **The London Inn** serves a good variety of meals and ales.

33 SIMONSBATH, EXE HEAD & CORNHAM FORD

Simonsbath in the heart of Exmoor is our start point for a stirring moorland and valley trek. After climbing through pastures beside **Lime Combe**, we go across the moorland plain at **Exe Head** enjoying fine views, then a short distance along **The Chains**. Our return is through a remote moorland stretch of the **Barle Valley** where there are few footpaths, giving us a sense of pioneering adventure as we find our way past **Cornham Ford** across rough Access Land. En route we pass centuries old mine workings where man has extracted iron and copper; after a steep ascent, wonderful views open up to the moors and along **Cornham Brake,** providing a fitting grand finale.

A GPS or compass should be carried on this route and the **Exe Head** area can be very wet and boggy after prolonged rain.

4   3¼H   9¼ miles/14.9km   370m / 370m   ↻   3*

* at **Simonsbath**

Extension
This route can be combined with two others for a longer moorland walk. At **Exe Head** Wp.8, join Route 30 Wp.8 to Wp.11 at **Woodbarrow Gate**; then join Route 36 from Wp.5 to Wp.10 near **Aclands Farm** and rejoin this route at Wp.12 (12.6 miles/20.3km, ascents & descents 420 metres).

Shorter route
To Wp.11 then left on the road to **Simonsbath** (6½ miles/10.5km, ascents & descents 210 metres).

Access by car: from **Lynton** (8 miles) and **Dulverton** (14 miles) take the B3223; from **Blackmoor Gate** (9 miles) take the A39, then B3358. Park in **Ashcombe** car park (SS 774394) above the **Exmoor Forest Inn**.

Heading back to the road from **Ashcombe** car park (Wp.1 0M) and turning right downhill to a junction, we bear left beside a restored Victorian Saw Mill onto the **South Molton** road. Going through a right hand gate before a bridge on a yellow-marked 'Exe Head via Lime Combe' (Wp.2 7M) path we criss-cross a *leat* over footbridges, stiles and along field slopes to a gate (Wp.3 17M). Bearing right across duckboards and a stile, we keep right to a gate, going right beside a 'Lime Combe' sign to a road. Crossing onto a blue-marked 'Exe Head Bridleway' (Wp.4 20M) on an ascending woodland track, we go through a gate to a 'bridleway through woods' sign (Wp.5 25M); bearing right, marker posts guide us between trees to a hedge and gate (Wp.6 31M).

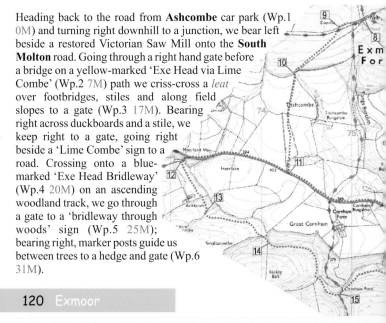

Big sheep country

Leaving the trees behind and entering large open pastures, we head into big sheep country following 'Exe Head' and 'Bridleway' signs; passing a marker post we stroll (N) near the top edge of **Lime Combe** aiming for a gate (Wp.7 46M) left of the animal pens, just below the skyline. It's fascinating to watch how quickly a modern day shepherd riding a quad bike can round up and pen his flock with the help of his traditional four legged friends.

Going through the gate and continuing along a right field edge (NNW), sweeping moorland views open up; passing through another gate, a 'Permitted Bridleway to Exe Head' sign points us diagonally left (NW) onto rougher moorland pasture dotted with reeds. Cresting **Exe Head**, there's no clear path in front, but keeping north-west, we aim for a wall and gate ahead, just left of the far valley. It's best to stay right of a boggy section on the gradual descent, then bear left beside the wall to the 'Exe Head' signpost (Wp.8 68M).

Our route on a 'Pinkery Pond and Cornham' track climbs gently through a gate, continuing for 'Pinkery' beside a wall to a 'B3358 via Titchcombe' sign (Wp.9 73M) that points us diagonally left down across the moor (SW). There is no clear path through rough grass as we drop around the top of **Bale Water** to our left and through a gate in a line of trees (Wp.10 84M).

The sign at Wp.9

Now striding out, our 'Bridleway to Cornham' crosses the middle of a large pasture, then over the next field (S) and through a sheep pen to a road (Wp.11 97M). Going gradually right downhill between beech hedges and taking care along the road, we pass **Moorland Cottage** then bear left onto a concrete farm track, crossing a bridge over the **River Barle** to a left hand signpost (Wp.12 112M).

The next 2½ miles offer superb hiking down the upper reaches of the beautiful remote **Barle Valley**; a permitted path leads us to **Exmoor National Park Access Land** from where we find our way to **Cornham Brake**. It's quite rough going and in places there are no paths but our efforts are rewarded with a marvellous winding valley landscape and a real sense of being off the beaten track. So, always keeping the river on our left, we set off on our expedition by following a 'Permitted Footpath to Cornham Ford' sign over the shoulder of a hill to a stile; continuing (SSE) down through long grass with an irrigation ditch on our right we cross a stile. The 'Permissive Footpath' marker directs us over a tiny stream and slightly left over the brow to a stile beside a gate (Wp.13 122M); crossing, we then bear left along a hillside track to climb above the valley. In this remote spot you are likely to see only buzzards wheeling above, a nonchalant lolloping fox or timid deer. At the hill top where the track swings right, we go straight on following the line of the river and after descending to the riverbank go through a gate onto ENP land where we can enjoy 'unlimited access on foot' (Wp.14 134M).

After picking our way along the riverbank at the foot of a steep slope we climb a rough animal path for 100 yards then strike off left along the hillside; there's no path but making our way through grass and heather we arrive at the top of a large bluff above the curving river.

... interlocking hills ...

Ahead, interlocking hills descend to the valley floor where we can see an interceptor across the **Barle** and on our right a stream runs down **Squallacombe**; finding a narrow path we descend to the riverbank. Fording or jumping over the tributary, then clambering over the interceptor pole (about the height of a field gate), we set off along the riverbank beside small crags and keeping to the right of a small reed bed pass a footbridge at **Cornham Ford** (Wp.15 154M).

Our route continues downstream into a broadening valley where a green sward covers hummocks and mounds of old mine workings; taking a rough narrow right hand path we climb along a low escarpment above the river. Crossing and re-crossing the line of an old stone wall we gradually descend across the slope towards the curves of **Cornham Brake** and the meandering river; a group of fir trees on the far bank camouflages the remains of mining activities. At the riverbank we find our way through reeds across two tributaries and around the base of a rocky knoll (Wp.16 171M). Although still on Access Land we are faced with a large reed bed where our choice is to strike right up a very steep slope to a gate onto a road (Wp.17 179M). This wonderful moorland and valley scene of **Cornham Brake** appears on many an Exmoor calendar.

Turning left down the road, we cross a bridge to a road junction; the large house opposite, once the residence of the Knight family, is now **The Simonsbath House Hotel**. Bearing right we climb the hill past - or perhaps into - **The Exmoor Forest Inn**, then on to the car park (Wp.18 196M).

34 SIMONSBATH, COW CASTLE & THE BARLE VALLEY

This route offers wild riverside scenery in the peaceful upper **Barle Valley**, set between flat topped moorland hills; a complete contrast to the landscape of reclaimed pastures we enjoy on our hilltop return.

The Knight family, based at **Simonsbath,** were instrumental in changing the face of central Exmoor during the 19th century; new farms were built and many acres of moors were cultivated, and miles of field boundaries were created from banks, topped with criss-crossing beech hedges acting as windbreaks. Our route passes two of the farms as well as a disused copper mine and an ancient Iron Age hill settlement.

On this straightforward route we stroll along well-established footpaths and tracks, clearly signed with blue paint; the outward riverside section is fairly level and there are two short uphill climbs on our return leg.

* at **Simonsbath, Exmoor Forest Inn** and **Boevey's Tea Rooms**

Access by car: from **Lynton** (8 miles) and **Dulverton** (14 miles) take the B3223; from **Blackmoor Gate** (9 miles) take the A39, then B3358. Park in **Ashcombe** car park (SS 774394) above **The Exmoor Forest Inn**.	**Stroll** Down the river valley as far as you like, returning along the same route. **Extension** On a 13¼ mile/21.3km trek (ascents & descents 570 metres), we can wade the **Barle** and join Walk 35 from **Landacre Bridge** to **Withypool**, rejoining this walk at Wp.5.

Starting from **Ashcombe** car park (Wp.1 0M) we walk back to the road and turn right down the pavement towards the **Exmoor Forest Inn**; crossing the road onto the 'Landacre via Picked Stones' bridleway, we climb through the trees to a path junction. Going straight on for 'Landacre via Cow Castle', our level well-trodden path runs along the side of the valley between beeches, once part of a tree nursery created by the Knight family. Leaving the dense wood through a gate with the river on our right, the valley opens out in front; immediately we feel miles from civilisation entering a wilder landscape of rough moorland pastures.

Our path, just above the valley floor

On our left, straight lines of mature beech trees grow out of the field boundary banks sweeping majestically down the slopes. Striding out through rapidly thinning trees we can see the line of our path just above the marshy valley floor, while the river below meanders between flat topped bare hills to disappear behind **Flexbarrow**. Curving up left behind the knoll beside the right hand wall, we go through a field gate then past cottage ruins to continue along the riverbank (Wp.2 21M); on the opposite bank over a footbridge is **Wheal Eliza**, a disused copper mine.

Strolling downstream, the next part of our route beside the river is particularly attractive; smooth rolling hills surround us as we walk under a stand of mature beeches, their branches gracefully arching over the water. Cutting across the bend of the river we head towards **Cow Castle** settlement, (Wp.3 41M) to climb around the hill beside a wall before swinging right between the **Cow** and the **Calf**.

... branches gracefully arching ...

A short detour clambering up the steep hillside past the ramparts to **Cow Castle's** summit gives us extensive views along the valley. Our path nears the river through grass and rushes as we cross a stile and footbridge (Wp.4 50M) to bear right on the flagstones to the riverbank where, ignoring the next footbridge, we follow the 'Withypool' sign into the conifers.

Approaching Wp.5

Passing the log barrier and following a wide forest track, we emerge through a gate onto the open hillside; our gradually ascending path enables us to appreciate the scale of the valley below, as we go through a field to a gate (Wp.5 65M).

For the extended walk to **Withypool**, turn right; 5 minutes downhill is a splendid picnic spot beside the **Barle**.

Our route now turns left up the moorland edge, parallel to the hedge bank, as we enjoy broad views of **Landacre Bridge** and down the valley to **Withypool**. At a sign for 'Simonsbath via Picked Stones' (Wp.6 77M) we turn left through the field to a gate in the far left hand corner, then bear left on a track to **Picked Stones Farm** (Wp.7 85M). From this point our 'Simonsbath' route is clearly marked, pointing along a track in front of the farm through two gates out into the fields; continuing beside hedge banks through several gates along the top of the hill.

On the slopes across the valley the field hedges of **Horsen Farm** look like huge green caterpillars crawling down the hillside.

Dropping to **White Water** past two metal gates, we climb to a signpost (Wp.8 105M); behind us there are views down the valley, while from this height, **Cow Castle** looks like a monk's tonsured head.

The field hedges of Horsen Farm

Passing a small copse on our right along the edge of two large fields we have a pleasant stroll (NW) between a hedge and a raised grass bank to the far end of a field, where we turn right beside a well-kept stone faced bank to the lane at **Winstitchen Farm** (Wp.9 122M).

Still in the fields, we bear diagonally left past a tin building and what looks like a raised golf tee, going straight on (NW) beside the right hand hedgerow to a gate, where the hedge switches to our left. Continuing in the same direction to a pond and small copse, then through the final field, we turn left into **Birchcleave Wood**.

We head downhill through mature woodlands with glimpses of **Simonsbath** below, to reach a path junction where we bear right for the road and car park (Wp.10 143M).

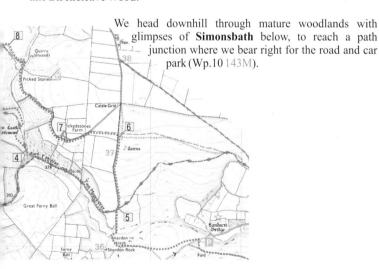

The popular summertime moorland haunt of **Landacre Bridge** provides simple leisure activities such as paddling in the **Barle** and relaxing on the river bank. It's also the start of a pleasant route to unspoilt **Withypool** village further downstream. Historically, **Landacre** was the site of a Swainmote Court that met here annually to deal with misdemeanours committed in the Royal Forest.

Our outward ramble runs along the moorland edge beside field boundaries; the Access Land to our right allows us to roam to **Brightworthy Barrow** or across to **Withypool Hill**. Returning along calming riverside paths and sunken lanes we saunter back down to **Landacre**, admiring the five solidly built medieval arches that have withstood both the ravages of time and the onslaught of many footballs.

* at **Withypool**

Extension

For a 13¼ mile/21.3km trek (ascents & descents 570 metres), complete this walk, then join Walk 34 to **Simonsbath** by wading the **Barle** upstream at **Sherdon Hutch**. From the upper car park, cross the road and head upstream, curving left along an escarpment above the right hand river. Going across a small gully, continue past rocky outcrops before finding your way down to the river bank at **Sherdon Hutch**. The return river crossing is at the same point; go straight ahead up the slope to a car park and turn left along a track. As the gradient eases, bear left alongside low mounds across the common and return to the car park. N.B. The river crossing should only be undertaken when the river is low.

Access by car: **Landacre Bridge** (SS816362) is 12 miles from **Dulverton** and 17 miles from **Lynton**; from **Chibbet Post** crossroads on the B3223 take a minor road (SW). Park in car parks near the bridge.

From the car park furthest from the river and with our back to the road (Wp.1 0M), we curve left across springy moorland grass, crossing a small stream at the foot of a hill to start our gradual ascent (ESE) on a wide track running beside low mounds. Climbing steadily along the hillside above the river we head for a signpost and gate beside a line of trees (Wp.2 11M); this is the point to which our route eventually returns.

Turning right beside a bank, we make our way up an indistinct path over rough moor for 6 minutes; the going can be wet in places up to the field corner. Bearing left along the field boundary we crest the hill as views open up ahead of **Withypool Hill**; our path goes gently left downhill and where the field edge kinks left we swing gradually right to rejoin a bank on the far side of the slope.

Staying beside a left hand boundary we cross a metalled lane (Wp.3 30M) heading downhill for 'Withypool', now clearly visible below are little white houses nestling amongst the trees. Suddenly in front of us is a steep sheltered *combe*; thankfully our path swings along the right hand slope rather than the near vertical face ahead!

Dropping to a fork, it's an easier descent on the right hand path rather than on the eroded water course to our left. This secluded valley rekindles memories of endless childhood days spent building dams – save the Pooh sticks for **Landacre Bridge**!

Crossing the stream and bearing left along the path, we tear ourselves away from this idyllic spot as our route climbs gently uphill through golden furze and beside a beech bank, gradually broadening into a track before reaching a lane (Wp.4 47M).

The tree-lined sunken lane

... through golden furze ...

Bearing left down the lane it's a short amble to the pretty riverside setting of **Withypool** and a welcome refreshment break at the Tea Rooms beside the 1960's Shell pumps, or further on at **The Royal Oak**.

Going back over the bridge, there's a signed river bank alternative path to **Landacre** that rejoins our route after the sunken lane.

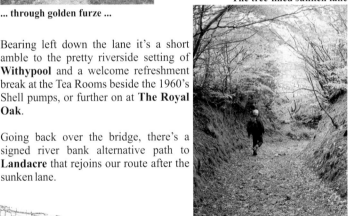

Our choice is to retrace our steps up the lane to Wp.4 (62M); walking beside the right hand hedge bank past an electricity pole we cross a stile to enter a lovely tree-lined sunken lane, going left at the end through a yellow-marked gate.

Strolling through pleasant meadows and rough pastures over stiles, footbridges and duckboards, we wind our way upstream along the riverbank. Swinging left away from the river, a 'Landacre' fingerpost (Wp.5 77M) directs us to another fingerpost, now spelt 'Lanacre' - to make things more confusing it's pronounced locally as "Lan-ak-er"!

The layered bank

Bearing slightly right and climbing between trees to **Brightworthy**, we pass through two gates, going right over a stile into a fenced corridor along a field edge to emerge onto a sunken lane. Turning right, stooping under beech branches, we climb a track beside a *layered bank*.

Landacre Bridge

If the ground is wet it's easier staying to the left of the track along field edges. After going through a gate and curving right to the brow of a hill, we head down to rejoin our outward route, (95M) striding out towards splendid moorland views and the distinctive profile of **Landacre Bridge** (106M).

A flowing moorland landscape is the setting for this relatively flat and straightforward route across the open spaces of **The Chains** on some of Exmoor's highest ground. There is a tremendous feeling of remoteness in what appears to be wild country; yet there are clues en route showing man's attempts to tame this terrain.

Starting with a steady climb through fields, we head along **The Chains**, the catchment for north and east Devon rivers, to a small reservoir at **Pinkery Pond**; turning south at **Woodbarrow** along the **Exmoor Royal Forest** boundary to **Mole's Chamber**, our return follows a Saxon military road.

There are blue waymarkings throughout the route but a GPS or compass should be carried in case of poor visibility. A short cut is available.

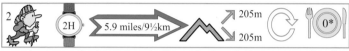

| 2 | 2H | 5.9 miles/9½km | | 205m / 205m | ↻ | 0* |

*nearest refreshments are in **Simonsbath** and **Challacombe** (3 miles)

Access by car: Park in B3358 roadside parking areas (SS 729401) between **Moorland Cottage** and the entrance to **Pinkery Farm Activity Centre**, 3 miles from **Simonsbath**, 6 miles from **Blackmoor Gate**.

Shorter walk
At Wp.4 turn left through a gate on a permitted path along the side of a *combe* then bear left past a wind turbine to the front of **Pinkery Farm Activity Centre**; go down a vehicle track to the B3358 at **Goat Bridge** and turn left along the verge (3.2 miles/5.1km, ascents & descents 100 metres).

From the parking area we go left through a gate (Wp.1 0M) on a blue-tipped 'Chains Barrow Bridleway', gradually climbing a large pasture parallel to a hedgebank. Continuing straight on through a second field, the terrain changes to rough grass mixed with reeds.

The source of the River Barle

After going through a gate (Wp.2 9M) we head north on a moorland path, guided up a gentle incline by a number of blue painted marker posts; half way, we cross two low canal banks running along the contour. Heading to the horizon and a fingerpost next to a gate (Wp.3 24M) our route turns left in front of a fence towards 'Pinkery Pond'; for a short detour to **Chains Barrow** and 360° views, follow the sign and footpath to the trig point, returning to Wp.3.

Enjoying fine vistas, we now stride out west along **The Chains** to a wall. After jinking right and left through a gate our gentle descent continues to **Pinkery**

Pinkery Pond and Canal

The small reservoir was constructed by the Knight family in the 19th century but historians have not discovered its exact purpose; it may simply have been for drainage and irrigation. However, a contour canal runs along the hillside, round **Exe Head** and on towards the river - possibly part of a grand design to power an inclined plane across the **Exe** as part of a mineral railway project.

Pond, (Wp.4 37M) the source of the **River Barle**. For the shorter route, turn left.

Crossing the dam and following the line of a wall up to a field corner, we go through a gate and bear diagonally right (NW) on a moorland path to a point where two walls meet at **Woodbarrow Gate** (Wp.5 50M), once an important intersection of moorland trails and ridge paths. The *barrow* lies behind the wall and from its summit there are sweeping views to **Longstone** and **Chapman Barrows** and beyond to **Wales**.

Turning left for the 'B3358 Road' and strolling along a wide track it's an easy descent towards a moorland ridge, whilst to our right a patchwork of fields leads the eye to the distant **North Devon** coast.

Going straight on through a gate and continuing near a right hand wall, we gradually curve left past cattle pens and through gates to a road (Wp.6 71M); this section from **Woodbarrow** runs along the county boundary between **Somerset** and **Devon** and was once the edge of the **Exmoor Royal Forest**.

Taking care crossing the road, our route along a 'Bridleway to Mole's Chamber' starts off down a rough track, then swings right uphill to the end of a tree line (Wp.7 77M). Bearing slightly left to 'Mole's Chamber' and keeping a post and wire fence on our right, we cross a soggy bit of ground; behind us lie the smooth slopes of **The Chains** and the dam wall of **Pinkery Pond**.

We head straight on through a gate (Wp.8 84M) to a field bottom, going through the right hand gate and along a rough pasture into a banked lane, to curve up to a track T-junction (Wp.9 95M). Opposite the grey **Sloley Stone** a 'Bridleway' sign points us sharp left on an ancient *herepath*; crossing a field and bearing right beside a wall past the mound of **Mole's Chamber**, our path descends over a stream and through a pedestrian gate.

The gate onto the rough pasture

The Herepath, passing Mole's Chamber

The **Herepath**, Saxon for 'army road', formed part of a network of military roads across southern England designed for speedy troop mobilisation to counter the threat of invading Danes; this was part of a route from the **Somerset Levels** through the **Quantocks** to **Simonsbath** then on to **Barnstaple** and **Cornwall**.

One myth surrounding **Mole's Chamber** suggests that a Reverend Mole (plus horse) was once swallowed up by a bog; another more prosaic explanation is that it was a dwelling – an 1891 census entry categorises **Mole's Chamber** as "vacant".

Our path runs along the side of a valley before winding its way over a hillock into a field; guided by low mounds we go down a rutted track onto a concrete farm lane (Wp.10 114M). Bearing left across a bridge over the embryonic **River Barle** we climb a few yards to the B3358 and turn left to our start point (Wp.11 121M).

37 BRENDON COMMON, BADGWORTHY WATER & FARLEY WATER

Brendon Common stretches south from **Shilstone Hill** to **Hoar Tor** along a broad moorland ridge, the four surrounding valleys each displaying their own distinct character and degree of remoteness. From **Brendon Two Gates** on the **Devon Somerset** border, our route crosses open moorland above **Hoccombe Water**, gradually descending to **Badgworthy Water** where a riverside path takes us down a charming valley past two fictional Doone locations. Climbing the quiet **Lankcombe** to an ancient ford, we re-cross **Brendon Common** and drop into **Farley Water**, a pretty but seldom walked valley where the rougher going requires some hillside scrambling before our final steady climb to the ridge.

A GPS or compass should be carried in case of poor visibility.

3/4 | 3H 20M | 8.9 miles/14.3km | 320m / 320m | ↻ | 0*

*nearest refreshments are in **Simonsbath** (3 miles)

Access by car: **Brendon Two Gates** on the Devon/Somerset border is in the middle of moorland on the B3223, 3 miles north of **Simonsbath** and 5 miles south-east of **Lynton**. Park in the large lay-by (SS 765432) immediately south of a cattle grid.

Shorter walk
From Wp.10 walk along B3223 road (7.4 miles/11.9km, ascents & descents 180 metres).

From Somerset, we go north over the cattle grid 'border' (Wp.1 0M) into Devon. Bearing right onto a broad grass path, we head (E) across open country, a relaxing start over a heather common, keeping the curved slopes of **Hoccombe Water** on our right all the way to **Badgworthy Water**. Descending gradually, widespread moorland views lie

A string of Exmoor ponies

ahead and grazing Exmoor ponies can often be seen; our way continues straight on (E) through a gate in a fence (Wp.2 21M) above the winding stream. Striding over a slight rise, the hills lining the far side of **Badgworthy Water** become more defined and to our right lie **Tom's Hill Barrows**; descending into a valley, we are surrounded by smooth slopes covered with bracken and grass. Our stony path passes a gate (Wp.3 44M) where its surface changes to grass; the attractive river lies on our right as we stroll downstream, climbing a short way before our undulating trail wends its way around rocky bluffs to a beech hedge.

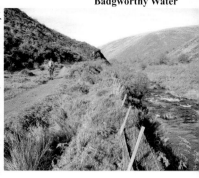

Bearing left, we walk the plank over a streamlet to go through a gate and climb the path ahead to a sign post. The hummocks to our left are the remains of a medieval settlement, perhaps the inspiration for Carver Doone's hideout in the novel Lorna Doone.

... a mass of purple rhododendrons ...

Going right for 'Cloud Farm and Oare' (Wp.4 57M) the valley starts to broaden and deepen; our path stays above the picturesque river for a while before entering a *sessile oak wood* and crossing a footbridge at the mouth of **Lankcombe**; in spring the right hand

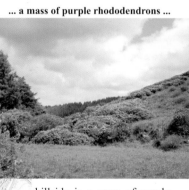

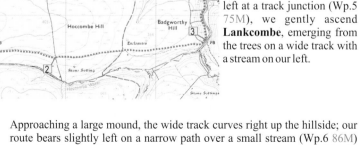

hillside is a mass of purple rhododendrons. On our left the smooth boulders in the stream are the supposed rock slide described in Lorna Doone.

Continuing for 200 yards into an open clearing and turning left at a track junction (Wp.5 75M), we gently ascend **Lankcombe**, emerging from the trees on a wide track with a stream on our left.

Approaching a large mound, the wide track curves right up the hillside; our route bears slightly left on a narrow path over a small stream (Wp.6 86M) then, ignoring another track to the right, we go straight on alongside the mound on our left, keeping in the main valley. A grass path between rocky knolls brings us to a fence and bank, where we turn sharp left downhill, then go right through a gate (Wp.7 92M) beside an interceptor on the stream bank. Our narrow grass path continues through heather and open moorland near the stream; this valley has a wild feel about it. Disturbing the occasional heron, we gradually climb to a centuries-old crossing point at **Lankcombe Ford** (Wp.8 110M) swinging right up a main track following conservation signs to a track intersection (Wp.9 113M).

Heading down to Farley Water

We go left (WSW) our level well-worn dirt track cresting **Brendon Common** where we are greeted with wide distant views to **Cheriton Ridge** and the coast. Bearing left along a road for 100 yards (Wp.10 132M) then curving right into bracken, we swing gradually right down a grass path along the top edge of a large gully towards **Farley Water**, aiming for a point where a path on the far hillside leaves the valley. Approaching the watercourse to the left of two hillocks (Wp.11 148M), we turn left above the bank, always keeping the stream on our right as we progress up this remote steep-sided valley.

The next section can't be rushed; our amble soon becomes a scramble after we swing left towards a large mound rising out of the valley floor. The path is very narrow and requires nimble footwork as we traverse a steep slope some 10 metres above tiny rapids and waterfalls; an alternative is to climb left up the slope onto higher ground rejoining the lower path beyond **Alse Barrow**.

Beyond the *barrow* we cross a tiny stream running down a gully from our left (Wp.12 164M); climbing slightly left for a short distance our path continues above **Farley Water** as we head past the two earthworks of **Holcombe Burrows** on our right. At the far end (Wp.13 173M), after passing several rivulets, the tranquil valley gently curves right; continuing on an easier distinct path we look for a point where a path comes slanting down the far right hand hillside to the stream bank and crosses to join our route. Continuing straight on at this junction (Wp.14 182M) our track soon leaves the main valley swinging left around **Clannon Ball** up a side *combe*; keeping the tributary on our right we steadily climb (E) to the valley top and ridge road (Wp.15 196M), turning right to the cattle grid (199M).

38 PORLOCK TO MINEHEAD via THE RUGGED COAST PATH

The National Trust has created a splendid trail along the cliff tops between **Porlock** and **Minehead**; stirringly described as the 'Rugged Alternative Coast Path', it offers excellent coastal hiking and fine views. The escarpment comprises hard *Hangman Sandstone* from the Middle Devonian geological period but erosion has created short deep valleys cutting down to the sea; the resulting roller-coaster path dips in and out of three *combes* between sections of springy open cliff tops.

After a level start across **Porlock Vale** and a strenuous ascent of **Hurlstone Combe**, the **Rugged Coast Path** winds its way to **North Hill** before a steady track descent to **Minehead**.

4 | 3H 20M | 9.1 miles/14.7km | 480m / 510m | !* | 4 **

* slight vertigo risk between **Western** and **Eastern Brockholes**
** in **Porlock** and **Minehead**

Shorter linear walk	**Extended circular walk from Porlock**	**Stroll**
At Wp.8 go straight on along acorn marked coast path and rejoin the route at Wp.14 (7.6 miles/12.2km, ascents 310 metres, descents 340 metres).	Turn right at Wp.14 along the acorn marked path returning to Wp.8 and back down **Hurlstone Combe** to **Porlock** (12.5 miles/20.1km, ascents & descents 520 metres).	- through fields to **Bossington** or **Hurlstone** and return.

Access by bus: First bus N°38 from **Minehead** and Quantock Motor Services N°300 coast bus from **Minehead**, **Combe Martin** and **Lynton/Lynmouth**.

Access by car: Porlock is on the A39, 6 miles from **Minehead** and 12 miles from **Lynmouth**. Car parks are in the village. Alternatively, park in the resort of **Minehead** and catch a bus to **Porlock**.

St. Dubricius Church (SS 886467) (Wp.1 0M) in the centre of **Porlock** marks our start point; facing the church we head left along the **High Street** then left again into **Sparkhayes Lane** (Wp.2 1M), strolling out of the village between several cottages. At the end of the tarmac, picking up a 'Bossington Coast Path' sign on our right, we climb a flight of steps and go along **Bay Road**, then turn left (Wp.3 9M).

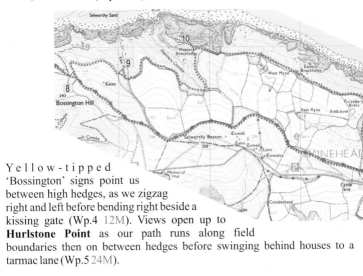

Y e l l o w - t i p p e d 'Bossington' signs point us between high hedges, as we zigzag right and left before bending right beside a kissing gate (Wp.4 12M). Views open up to **Hurlstone Point** as our path runs along field boundaries then on between hedges before swinging behind houses to a tarmac lane (Wp.5 24M).

Going right past a row of flowery cottages into the pretty village of **Bossington** and bearing left onto a National Trust 'Bridleway to Hurlstone Point' we cross **Horner Water** on an arched footbridge, keeping left for 'Hurlstone Point' (Wp.6 28M). Emerging from trees through a gate onto Access Land, our clear track starts its gradual ascent giving us views over the shingle ridge towards **Porlock Bay**; arriving at a National Trust sign we go right on a 'Minehead' path (Wp.7 42M).

Down Hurlstone Combe and across Porlock Bay

After crossing a path junction the gradient steepens as we traipse up an unforgiving stone-studded path, there are no twists and turns, our route just goes straight up the middle of a bare *combe*; frequent pauses enable us to enjoy an increasingly grand vista of **Porlock Bay** and distant cliffs.

Nearing the top and continuing straight on past a bench we soon arrive at a 'Rugged Alternative Coastpath' sign (Wp.8 63M); taking this more adventurous route to **Minehead**, we bear sharp left off the official coast path - the shorter linear walk continues straight on.

Sauntering along a broad grass track and curving right around a moorland edge, there are splendid views across the **Bristol Channel** to the line of the Welsh coast and silhouetted **Brecon Beacons**; grass covered cliffs fall away to our left at a gentle angle, rather than dropping vertically. Descending into **East Combe** and forking left (Wp.9 72M) on a narrow path, we cross the top end of the valley, swinging left through a gate to the cliff tops.

For the next three miles we can put this book away to enjoy a diversity of flora and fauna and dramatic ever-changing views along this remote coastline.

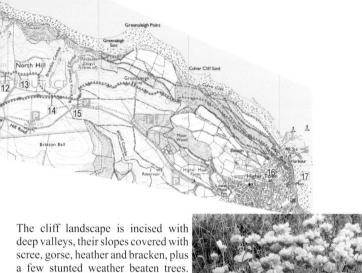

The cliff landscape is incised with deep valleys, their slopes covered with scree, gorse, heather and bracken, plus a few stunted weather beaten trees. Stonecrop, thrift and thyme cling to ledges and dry stone walls; the area also provides nesting habitats for ravens and peregrine falcons.

The undulating path to Furzebury Brake

A bright patch of thrift

Our route bends inland descending into **Henners Combe**, then crosses a stream before we regain height to a headland at **Western Brockholes** (Wp.10 100M) and bear right along the top of steep slopes; taking care over rocky outcrops our undulating path continues beside field walls to **Furzebury Brake** headland (Wp.11 128M). Here, the circular ramparts of an Iron Age enclosure stand at the summit of a field on our right; appreciating this fine defensive position, we descend steeply into **Grexy Combe** and after twisting our way down to a stream, curve left up a little wild valley. At marker posts, our path goes left over a stream (Wp.12 144M) then right up to a stile and gate beside a National Trust Information Board; going straight across an intersection (Wp.13 147M) on a grass path (E) we gradually bear right through the bracken to a track T-junction (Wp.14 154M).

Turning left along **North Hill**, an acorn marked coast path leads us to a car park and sign post (Wp.15 158M); the first left hand path is our route for 'Minehead Harbour' as we head down between gorse bushes before bearing right on a track along the coast. Our steady woodland descent wends along the cliffs and after ignoring right and left paths, the stony trail eventually becomes a tarmac lane; as we exit the National Park there are glimpses far below of the harbour.

Joining a road, we keep left for 25 yards then turn left (Wp.16 192M) at a small yellow marker down a tarmac path, negotiating hairpin bends and following acorn symbols; bearing left downhill and descending steps, we enter a narrow lane dropping to an impressive sculpture on the sea front (Wp.17 200M). This marks the start and finish of the 630-mile **South West Coast Path** from **Minehead** to **Poole Harbour** in **Dorset**, the longest of the UK's long distance trails.

From here, turning right, it's a short stroll beside the sea wall to the car parks or the **Porlock** bus stop beside the railway station. Incidentally the last section from **North Hill** was completed at a fast lick and reflects the time recorded; helpful perhaps if, like us, you also have to catch the last bus!

39 DUNSTER, WITHYCOMBE & BAT'S CASTLE

Dunster is a favourite tourist attraction, delightfully set on the northern fringe of Exmoor with a backdrop of hills and valleys. The quaint streets and buildings of this bustling large village are dominated by an ancient castle and **St. George's Church**, as well as other historic features including a **Yarn Market**, and working **Water Mill**.

The castle's deer park is the setting for the outward part of our route, followed by a stroll across quiet fields and farm tracks to the village of **Withycombe**. Our one long climb takes us high along a ridge, much of which is **Access Land**, to visit two early Iron Age hill forts; excellent vantage points to appreciate fine coastal and inland scenery.

2/3   2½ H   6.8 miles/11km   320m / 320m   4*

***Dunster**

Access by bus: First bus Nº398 **Minehead - Dulverton - Tiverton**.

Access by car: **Dunster** is 3 miles from **Minehead** on the A396; ½ mile from the junction with A39. Park in the car park by the Information Centre (SS 993439).

Short walk
At Wp.3, turn right up the track to 'Withycombe Hill Gate'. At top of hill, re-join the walk just after Wp.11, turning right on 'Dunster bridleway', then straight on to 'Bats Castle settlement' (4.1 miles/6.6km, ascents & descents 220 metres).

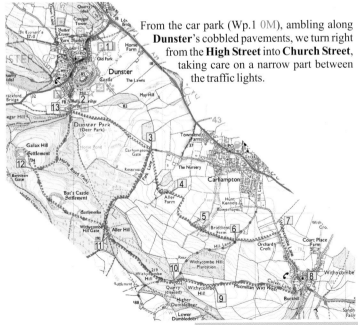

From the car park (Wp.1 0M), ambling along **Dunster**'s cobbled pavements, we turn right from the **High Street** into **Church Street**, taking care on a narrow part between the traffic lights.

Gallox Bridge

Continuing down to a no through road sign and bearing left into **Mill Lane**, we walk beside a *leat* for a short distance, then go right on a tarmac path signed 'Packhorse Bridge'.

Dunster Castle

At a T-junction, we turn left between pretty thatched cottages and over the medieval **Gallox Bridge**, heading up a track to a path crossroads (Wp.2 15M). Bearing left for 'Carhampton' through a kissing gate and forking immediately left, we gradually climb a well trodden public footpath with **Dunster Castle** behind us and low level coastal views across **Blue Anchor Bay** to our left.

Our undulating grass path runs beside a fence through the old **Deer Park**, going through one gate, then continuing to another at the brow of a field, where we emerge onto a track (Wp.3 29M). For a shorter walk turn right uphill on a red marked 'RUPP to Withycombe Hill Gate'.

Our route from here to **Withycombe** is not signed; a couple of paces to our right, on the other side of the track, a narrow path is concealed in the undergrowth. Going down shallow steps we cross a stile in the hedge, heading diagonally right over a large field; aiming for a gap in the far hedge to the right of a barn, we join a track curving left between outbuildings at **Aller Farm**.

Opposite the last left hand black barn is a double metal gate (Wp.4 38M); we go right and immediately left along the field edge, through a gate and turn right beside a hedge to a field corner. Climbing over a fixed gate and swinging left towards the start of a farm track, we skirt a patch of nettles and brambles, going along the track between hedges.

Looking back to Briddicott Farm

As **Briddicott Farm** comes into view piles of rubble lie ahead; bypassing the track, we go right through a gate (Wp.5 47M) and left along the field edge to the farm buildings. Going straight on between them up a little used grass track to a T-junction (Wp.6 55M), we turn left for 20 yards then right over a stile set into the bank, strolling down the length of a field along the **Exmoor National Park** boundary. Bearing right up a lane (Wp.7 62M) to **Withycombe** our route goes right for 'Dunster' at the top of a rise (Wp.8 68M); the white washed **Church of St Nicholas**, a 100 yards further down the lane, is worth a visit to see the beautifully kept stone interior and fine 15th century Rood screen.

Slogging doggedly up a steep lane, the tarmac soon peters out as our earth and stone track heads between high banks through a gate and onto rough pastures; beside the track a millennium stone has been erected by the parishioners of **Withycombe** and **Rodhuish**. Their lasting commemoration on this hillside is a large ring of twenty beeches, one per century, plus a welcoming bench for hikers to relax and enjoy good coastal scenes. Heading upwards, the gradient thankfully eases; crossing a stile (Wp.9 87M), our views are now inland as we walk beside a right hand fence towards the gorse covered mound of **Withycombe Hill**, where a warning fire beacon once stood.

At a gate, the Access Symbol indicates that we are free to roam the land along the ridge; our level route crosses a track junction (Wp.10 93M) as we stride straight on between gorse bushes through a gate and into a wood. Continuing ahead over a forest trail junction to a fork (Wp.11 107M), we bear right to a track junction in front of the **Kings Hedge** - a substantial beech hedge bank marking the Deer Park boundary.

... between gorse bushes ...

Bearing left through a gap in the bank towards 'Dunster', we immediately head straight on into a belt of trees, along a yellow-marked permitted path to 'Bat's Castle'. Coming into another open Access Area our heather edged path climbs gently to an impressive Iron Age circular hill fort; the defensive double ramparts and deep ditch can be clearly seen, and an information board explains what life was like for the inhabitants. From both here and **Gallax Hill** further along the ridge, there are extensive views to **Croydon**, **Dunkery** and **Grabbist Hills** as well as **Dunster** and the castle.

Our path continues downhill through patches of bracken and *whortleberries* to a *saddle* (Wp.12 122M) where we turn right to start our ridge descent on a grass path. For a 5 minute detour to a second hill fort on the summit of **Gallax Hill**, go straight on and return to this point. Forking left after 1 minute on a narrow path, we slither our way down the steep wooded hillside, bearing left onto a stony track, then left at a signpost to rejoin our outward route (Wp.13 134M). Going through the kissing gate and re-crossing the **River Avill,** we retrace our way past **Dunster**'s many refreshment opportunities to the car park (148M).

Thatched cottages in Dunster

This route through **Porlock Vale** offers an interesting variety of level meadows, hillside paths, and mature woods. Starting inland from **Horner** we head seawards down a wide valley towards the dominating presence of **Bossington Hill**. A short climb gives wonderful views across **Porlock Bay** and along wooded cliffs before reaching **Hurlstone Point** from where we can admire the unique pebble ridge which stretches across the bay. Since the ridge was breached by storms it now only partially protects the vale from high tides and as a result a salt marsh habitat is being naturally created.

After an invigorating stomp along the shingle ridge, our route follows level paths into the large village of **Porlock**; a sharp road climb gives us glimpses of the vale before a final bridleway descent via a packhorse bridge to **Horner**. If sea conditions are too rough, the return route is straight on at Wp.8 to 'Bossington', then along a 'Porlock footpath' to Wp.12.

2 | 2¼ H | 6½ miles/10½km | 200m / 200m | ↻ | 3*

*in **Porlock**, **Horner**

Access by bus: None to **Horner**; though by using the N°38 or N°300 bus service, **Porlock** is an alternative start and finish point.

Access by car: **Horner** car park (SS 898456) is 1 mile south of **Red Post** junction between **Porlock** and **Allerford** on A39.

> **Shorter Walk**
> At Wp.4, continue along the lane through **Bossington** and turn left on a 'Porlock footpath' to rejoin the route at Wp.12 (4¼ miles/6.8km ascents & descents 110 metres).

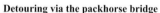

Detouring via the packhorse bridge

Turning right out of the main car park exit (Wp.1 0M), it's a relaxing start along a level lane beside **Horner Water** before detouring over a small packhorse bridge on our left. We then rejoin the lane and continue straight on at a road junction towards **Minehead** (Wp.2 8M). After **West Luccombe Farm**, where the lane bends left, we go ahead along a track signed 'Footpath A39 road Bossington', entering a pasture and following a well defined path to the main road.

Turning right and carefully crossing **New Bridge**, we immediately bear left across a field on a yellow-marked 'Bossington Footpath' (Wp.3 14M) and through a gate into a wood. Our path curves right then left to a gate in the tree line. Emerging into meadows and strolling left along a clear path, we go through two gates before swinging right to a lane; it's easy walking with pleasant views across **Porlock Vale** to the houses snuggled along the foot of

Bossington Hill.

Going left along the lane then right over a stone bridge (Wp.4 27M) on a 'Selworthy Beacon Bridleway'(the shorter walk continues along the lane), our route ascends a tarmac track between cottages before bearing left on a woodland path. Going straight on at the first path junction, we shortly arrive at a signpost, keeping right for 'Selworthy Beacon' (Wp.5 31M). Climbing **Lynch Combe** into **Allerford Woods** beside a stream, we come to a path crossroads (Wp.6 35M); turning left for 'Hurlstone' our contouring path runs in ancient woods before swinging left through a gate beside a dry stone wall.

... lovely views open up ...

As we clear the trees, lovely views open up across the vale and along the steep wooded cliffs from **Porlock Weir** to **Foreland Point**. Our path gradually descends across the side of **Bossington Hill** to the foot of **Hurlstone Combe** (Wp.7 54M).

We continue straight on over a path crossroads to **Hurlstone Point**, where the derelict coastguard lookout provides broad views over the **Bristol Channel**.

Retracing our steps to the first path fork, we bear right, then turn right onto an unsigned path (Wp.8 63M), crossing a stile and descending stone steps to the ridge that protects **Porlock Bay** from the **Bristol Channel**. Turning left and tramping along the shingle beach, we either lean into buffeting westerlies or are cooled by zephyrs; two sets of wooden posts driven into the pebbles mark the point where **Horner Water** flows under the ridge (Wp.9 79M).

Just beyond the second line of posts we bear left on a small yellow-marked grass path running parallel to the beach between ruined WWII defences. At a kissing gate behind a lime kiln (Wp.10 82M), we follow directions for 'Porlock Weir via Marsh', diagonally left across a field then through a gate and over a footbridge. Now walking beside a right hand hedge and ignoring a path to 'Porlock Weir', we go ahead on a 'Bossington Porlock' path to a path T-junction. Turning right along a 'Permissive Path'(Wp.11 87M), we march across fields along a broad grass track, left, right, left, switching from side to side of the hedgerow, before going through a pedestrian gate. An enclosed path between tall hedges brings us to **Bay Road** (Wp.12 98M); keeping right following a 'Porlock' sign to the end of the housing estate, we go down a short flight of steps and turn left into **Sparkhayes Lane**. Gently wending our way up between cottages to the centre of **Porlock**, we turn right at the **High Street** T-junction (Wp.13 106M) to **St. Dubricius Church**; this busy village has a variety of shops, tea rooms and an Information Centre.

Leaving Porlock along The Drang

Turning left beside the church gates along a tarmac alleyway called **The Drang** and forking right between stone walls beside a nursery, we go through a gate onto **Coach Road**, keeping left of the bungalows to a T-junction. Going right up **Doverhay Lane** then keeping left for 'West Luccombe', we climb steeply out of **Porlock** along the edge of **Doverhay Wood Access Land** with good views across the vale towards the coast.

After passing a cattle grid and road junction, the lane starts to descend; forking right (Wp.14 124M) onto a 'Horner Bridlepath' and ignoring the higher 'Granny's Ride' sign, we meander down through the trees as our path swings right then left through a gate before dropping to a cobbled pack horse bridge across **Horner Water** (Wp.15 136M). Turning left along the lane for a few paces we re-enter the car park on our right; seasonal tea rooms lie along a path beside the information board and toilets.

Porlock Ridge and Salt Marsh

A shingle ridge forming the beach in front of **Porlock Vale** protects it from the **Bristol Channel** which has the second highest tidal rise and fall in the world; strong currents and westerly winds produce a *longshore drift*, causing pebbles to be gradually moved along the beach from **Porlock Weir** to **Hurlstone Point**.

In 1996, battered by storms, the ridge was breached near **Porlock Weir**; rather than attempting a repair, the large gap was left, allowing nature to take its course.

A section behind the ridge is regularly flooded creating a new salt marsh habitat that attracts waders and migrating birds. The whole area is a Site of Special Scientific Interest providing a unique opportunity to monitor the effect of rising sea levels.

THE EXMOOR FOREST PERAMBULATION – AN ORGANISED 31 MILE TREK

What do you say when a friend asks if you would like to take part in the annual organised walk around the perimeter of the **Exmoor Royal Forest** in mid June? After 27 miles on a very hot Saturday and with sore feet you realise that the answer should have been a resounding " NO"! But 4 miles later as you climb the final slope to claim your badge and certificate it 's more like, "Well, that was certainly some challenge"

Is it worth undertaking this day long trek, first started in 1279, around these ancient royal boundaries? Depends on how much of a masochist you are because there are some really tough sections, including a near vertical climb out of the **Exe Valley**, two boggy tussocky plodding bits and a final 7½ mile grind along Devon lanes.

On the plus side you'll see some splendid private hidden parts of the moor, open only for this walk. In particular the views up **Exe Cleave** are absolutely magnificent and take your breath away, although that's probably the effect of the ascent as well!

Most efficiently run by the Exmoor Youth Association in conjunction with ENP, the perambulation starts at 7.30 am from **Pinkery Exploration Centre** SS723411. The clockwise route goes via **Pinkery Pond** to **Woodbarrow**, then north to **Saddle Gate**, the first of 7 checkpoints. We turn east to **Brendon Two Gates** going in and out of several deep valleys and then it's a level walk to **Badgworthy Water**.

After a steep climb onto **South Common** we drop down into pretty **Chalk Water** then rise steadily to **Black Barrow**, swinging south over tough open moor to **Alderman's Barrow**. There is a short section of road to **Larkbarrow** corner where we descend **Sparcombe**, then wade the **Exe** and clamber up to the halfway check point at **Picked Stones Lane**.

Heading south across the moor we ford the **Barle** and climb up to **Landacre Gate** and **Hawkridge Common**, slogging across **Halscombe Allotment** past **Willingford Farm** to **White Post** before starting the long grinding road section. Our mainly level route is north-west past **Kinsford Gate** to **Mole's Chamber** with excellent views south-west over **Barnstaple Bay**. The final bridleway leads north over moor bringing the welcome sight of the finish at **Pinkery** and a very well-earned rest.

Refreshments - water provided en route!
Information and web sites listed in the Appendices under Useful Information

A TIP - You'll be wading two rivers; if you want to keep your boots dry use a pair of cheap aqua shoes.

A FINAL TIP - a welcoming support team at later checkpoints really helps during this long day.

See the notes on **Using GPS on Exmoor** on page 16.

GPS RECEPTION AND ANOMALIES

GPS reception is good on most routes, particularly moors, surrounding farmland and the coastline. Reception can be poor or intermittent on the floors or sides of steep valleys; the majority are short stretches with signed paths and tracks. The routes with the longest sections of poor reception are 9, 16, 20, 25 and 29, all along wooded valley floors and slopes and following clear paths.

Routes affected are:

2	Wps.14-15	15	Wps.1-2 Wps.11-12	27	Wp.5 -Tarr Steps
5	Wps. 5-6 Wps. 13-14	16	Wps. 2-3 Wp.7- Lynmouth	28	Wps. 5-6 Wps.10-11
7	Wps. 6-7	19	Wps.10-11 Wps.13-14	29	Wp. 4-5 Wp.9 - Lynmouth
8	Wps. 2-4	20	Wps.11-14	30	Wps. 2-3
9	Wps. 4-5 Wp.14-Porlock outskirts	22	Wps. 2-3	33	Wps. 4-5 Wps.14-15
		23	Wps. 5-6	37	Wps. 3-4
13	Wps.1-2	25	Wps. 7-9 Wps.11-12	40	Wps. 5-6 Wps.14-15
14	Wps.3-4 Wps.7-8	26	Wp.3 - Kennel Farm		

1
HUNTER'S INN & WOODY BAY

Wp	Zo	East	North
1	SS	65523	48071
2	SS	65523	48248
3	SS	66243	49423
4	SS	66307	49353
5	SS	67373	48661
6	SS	67994	48764
7	SS	67508	48895
B	SS	67691	48981
8	SS	67206	48978
9	SS	65494	49025
10	SS	65514	48133

2
SELWORTHY, BOSSINGTON & ALLERFORD

Wp	Zo	East	North
1	SS	91990	46786
2	SS	91971	47192
3	SS	92351	47363
4	SS	92618	47617
5	SS	92317	47894
6	SS	91551	48018
7	SS	91144	48220
8	SS	90443	48714
9	SS	90155	49024
10	SS	89958	49196
11	SS	89979	48933
12	SS	90052	48186
13	SS	89798	47987
14	SS	90073	47615
15	SS	90377	47099
16	SS	90719	46859
17	SS	91952	46821

3
SELWORTHY & NORTH HILL - A PANORAMIC SPLENDOUR

Wp	Zo	East	North
1	SS	91948	46822
2	SS	92010	47249
3	SS	92346	47365
4	SS	92620	47621
5	SS	93243	47637
6	SS	93567	47577
7	SS	94771	47689
8	SS	93944	47648
9	SS	92523	48288
10	SS	91557	48014
11	SS	91889	47993
12	SS	91511	47704
13	SS	91518	47285
14	SS	91687	47182
15	SS	91711	46888
16	SS	91945	46942
17	SS	91960	46828

4
STOKE PERO COMMON & DUNKERY BEACON

Wp	Zo	East	North
1	SS	87875	42690
2	SS	89139	42408
3	SS	89164	41599
4	SS	87538	41536
5	SS	87077	41896
6	SS	86566	42852
7	SS	86741	43250
8	SS	87732	42978
9	SS	87877	42715

5
HORNER, STOKE PERO & WEBBER'S POST

Wp	Zo	East	North
1	SS	89771	45566
2	SS	89659	44002
3	SS	89484	43724
4	SS	88762	43868
5	SS	88287	44107
6	SS	87373	43370
7	SS	87844	43544
8	SS	88291	43770
9	SS	88501	43759
10	SS	88597	43651
11	SS	89580	43377
12	SS	89867	43520
13	SS	89814	43713
14	SS	90003	43760
15	SS	90178	44163
16	SS	90298	44395
17	SS	89974	44952
18	SS	89828	45451

6
WINSFORD, WINSFORD HILL & PUNCHBOWL

Wp	Zo	East	North
1	SS	90602	34903
2	SS	90513	34665
3	SS	90421	33869
4	SS	90507	33521
5	SS	90553	33159
6	SS	90300	33258
7	SS	88937	33732
8	SS	88973	33561
9	SS	88694	33461
10	SS	88123	33868

(continued)

Wp	Zo	East	North
11	SS	87613	34091
12	SS	88160	34189
13	SS	88618	35098
14	SS	90146	35091
15	SS	90597	34895

7
WINSFORD CIRCULAR via BYE COMMON & THE EXE VALLEY

Wp	Zo	East	North
1	SS	90609	34910
2	SS	90021	35221
3	SS	89687	35578
4	SS	89134	35820
5	SS	88672	35785
6	SS	88195	36060
7	SS	87684	36105
8	SS	89461	36234
9	SS	90084	35144
10	SS	90605	34907

8
TARR STEPS & WINSFORD HILL

Wp	Zo	East	North
1	SS	87185	32364
2	SS	86721	32110
3	SS	85955	32760
4	SS	85722	33948
5	SS	86103	34428
6	SS	86316	34458
7	SS	86832	34509
8	SS	87613	34090
9	SS	88161	34185
10	SS	88723	34204
11	SS	88840	33558
12	SS	89725	33007
13	SS	89389	32210
14	SS	89028	32096
15	SS	88110	31747
16	SS	86815	32131

9
PORLOCK, PITTCOMBE HEAD & HAWK COMBE

Wp	Zo	East	North
1	SS	88534	46849
2	SS	88376	46750
3	SS	88131	46761
4	SS	86986	46897
5	SS	86724	47298
6	SS	86431	47887
7	SS	85896	48119
8	SS	85219	47289
9	SS	84638	46993
10	SS	84125	46255
11	SS	85558	46447
12	SS	85580	46234
13	SS	86449	45643

(continued)

Wp	Zo	East	North
14	SS	86737	45561
15	SS	88620	46701
16	SS	88536	46853

10
EXFORD, ROOM HILL & THE EXE VALLEY

Wp	Zo	East	North
1	SS	85476	38358
2	SS	85747	38040
3	SS	85653	37923
4	SS	85914	37246
5	SS	85557	36721
6	SS	85658	36289
7	SS	86153	36114
8	SS	86904	36250
9	SS	87622	36143
10	SS	87212	36104
11	SS	87159	36231
12	SS	86816	37543
13	SS	86358	37853
14	SS	85509	38311

11
ROMANCING WITH LORNA DOONE - ROBBER'S BRIDGE, OARE & DOONE VALLEY

Wp	Zo	East	North
1	SS	82107	46483
2	SS	80216	47332
3	SS	80064	47039
4	SS	79426	46740
5	SS	79133	45311
6	SS	79288	44489
7	SS	79568	43737
8	SS	80079	43238
9	SS	80903	43341
10	SS	80583	44253
11	SS	80881	44968
12	SS	82086	46473

12
COMBE MARTIN, HOLDSTONE HILL & THE HANGMANS

Wp	Zo	East	North
1	SS	57773	47279
2	SS	57885	47130
3	SS	57995	47188
4	SS	58142	47132
5	SS	58894	47058
6	SS	59834	47080
7	SS	61026	46593
8	SS	61912	46855
9	SS	62401	47403
10	SS	61949	47709
11	SS	61298	47740
12	SS	61213	47804
13	SS	61240	47606

(continued)

Wp	Zo	East	North
14	SS	60393	47750
15	SS	60081	48071
16	SS	58610	48012
17	SS	57731	47582
18	SS	57771	47341

13
STARK CONTRASTS! HEDDON VALLEY & HOLDSTONE HILL

Wp	Zo	East	North
1	SS	65533	48057
2	SS	65450	48825
3	SS	65489	49576
4	SS	65404	48889
5	SS	65433	48623
6	SS	65245	49423
7	SS	64901	49149
8	SS	63465	48319
9	SS	62390	48019
10	SS	61218	47802
11	SS	61301	47742
12	SS	61952	47708
13	SS	62530	47681
14	SS	63062	47251
15	SS	63602	46996
16	SS	64240	47952
17	SS	65506	48137

14
WHEDDON CROSS, DUNKERY BEACON & DUNSTER

Wp	Zo	East	North
1	SS	92393	38774
2	SS	93290	39461
3	SS	93263	39672
4	SS	92291	39760
5	SS	92150	39883
6	SS	91870	39975
7	SS	91627	39937
8	SS	90912	40507
9	SS	90360	40587
10	SS	89564	40629
11	SS	89170	41582
12	SS	90400	42037
13	SS	90703	42244
14	SS	92860	43131
15	SS	93988	43450
16	SS	94628	44139
17	SS	94896	44215
18	SS	96065	43929
19	SS	97936	43706
20	SS	98776	43494
21	SS	99154	43886

15
ROADWATER, NETTLECOMBE & MONKSILVER CIRCULAR

Wp	Zo	East	North
1	ST	03138	38241
2	ST	03400	37992
3	ST	03892	37834
4	ST	04046	37803
5	ST	04313	37647
6	ST	05075	37558
7	ST	05738	37782
8	ST	06342	38424
9	ST	06836	37875
10	ST	07320	37470
11	ST	07030	37023
12	ST	05375	36108
13	ST	04666	36303
14	ST	04522	36532
15	ST	03224	38186

16
LYNMOUTH, WATERSMEET & COUNTISBURY

Wp	Zo	East	North
1	SS	72248	49656
2	SS	72416	49493
3	SS	74721	49044
4	SS	74463	49508
5	SS	74728	49635
6	SS	74702	49800
7	SS	73073	49524
8	SS	72246	49625

17
LYNTON & THE VALLEY OF ROCKS

Wp	Zo	East	North
1	SS	71891	49499
2	SS	71437	49205
3	SS	71274	49227
4	SS	70291	49330
5	SS	70097	49161
6	SS	69571	48959
7	SS	69826	49191
8	SS	70535	49733
9	SS	71081	49951
10	SS	72030	49589
11	SS	71908	49509

18
COUNTING THE COMBES TO COUNTISBURY

Wp	Zo	East	North
1	SS	75268	49661
2	SS	75467	49800
3	SS	75681	49725
4	SS	75892	49635
5	SS	76356	49691
6	SS	76876	49629
7	SS	77443	49032
8	SS	78199	48839
9	SS	78450	49279
10	SS	77967	49600
11	SS	77051	49929
12	SS	76142	50208
13	SS	75938	50334
14	SS	75849	50359
15	SS	75585	50464
16	SS	75443	51083
17	SS	75061	50611
18	SS	75008	50383
19	SS	74747	49864

19
LYNTON PARRACOMBE & WOODY BAY

Wp	Zo	East	North
1	SS	71872	49495
2	SS	71565	49220
3	SS	69992	47490
4	SS	67898	47331
5	SS	67747	46941
6	SS	67379	45963
7	SS	66961	44974
8	SS	66080	45417
9	SS	65831	46745
10	SS	65512	48128
11	SS	65742	49622
12	SS	67222	48978
13	SS	68870	49049
14	SS	69826	49193
15	SS	70550	49780
16	SS	71901	49499

20
ROBBER'S BRIDGE, PORLOCK WEIR, CULBONE & BROOMSTREET FARM

Wp	Zo	East	North
1	SS	82111	46478
2	SS	82725	46979
3	SS	83103	47110
4	SS	83292	47211
5	SS	83544	47267
6	SS	84090	47125
7	SS	84633	46988
8	SS	85211	47279
9	SS	86371	47333
10	SS	86724	47294
11	SS	86432	47887
12	SS	85028	48290
13	SS	84174	48201
14	SS	83874	48247
15	SS	82273	48185
16	SS	81087	48417
17	SS	81079	47813
18	SS	81444	46560
19	SS	82102	46472

21
WHEDDON CROSS TO DUNSTER via THE LOST VILLAGE OF CLICKET

Wp	Zo	East	North
1	SS	92383	38759
2	SS	92991	38847
3	SS	93183	37933
4	SS	94107	37265
5	SS	95033	37143
6	SS	95529	37068
7	SS	96081	37190
8	SS	97136	38066
9	SS	96850	38690
10	SS	96231	39528
11	SS	95574	42112
12	SS	96631	42072
13	SS	97620	42279
14	SS	98960	43106
15	SS	99157	43809

22
THE LUXBOROUGH VALLEY & WITHYCOMBE COMMON

Wp	Zo	East	North
1	SS	98464	37648
2	SS	98504	37376
3	SS	97728	37514
4	SS	97423	37923
5	SS	98047	38489
6	SS	98353	38771
7	SS	98376	39370
8	SS	99188	39579
9	SS	99466	38953
10	SS	99848	38062
11	SS	99058	37826
12	SS	98453	37693

23
RALEGH'S CROSS, COMBERROW & STICKLEPATH

Wp	Zo	East	North
1	ST	03541	34366
2	ST	03142	34304
3	ST	02642	34755
4	ST	02529	34745
5	ST	02134	35451
6	ST	02058	35818
7	ST	02962	35444
8	ST	02892	35314
9	ST	03714	36467
10	ST	03731	36537
11	ST	04528	36527
12	ST	04563	36071
13	ST	04648	35131
14	ST	04080	34788
15	ST	03544	34368

24
HAWKRIDGE CIRCULAR via ANSTEY GATE

Wp	Zo	East	North
1	SS	86063	30697
2	SS	85925	31306
3	SS	85641	31730
4	SS	84761	31267
5	SS	84578	31165
6	SS	84404	31106
7	SS	84082	31051
8	SS	83760	30725
9	SS	83503	29813
10	SS	84562	29860
11	SS	85164	29998
12	SS	85804	30122
13	SS	85565	30357
14	SS	86002	30677

25
DULVERTON, HINAM CROSS & THE BARLE VALLEY

Wp	Zo	East	North
1	SS	91236	27921
2	SS	91055	27955
3	SS	90677	28042
4	SS	90159	28034
5	SS	89168	28559
6	SS	89031	28563
7	SS	88347	29030
8	SS	88358	29332
9	SS	88352	29648
10	SS	88159	29792
11	SS	88298	29768
12	SS	90677	28929
13	SS	90570	28740
14	SS	91232	27834

26
DULVERTON MARSH BRIDGE COURT DOWN

Wp	Zo	East	North
1	SS	91231	27833
2	SS	91059	27968
3	SS	90675	28517
4	SS	90690	28931
5	SS	90780	28964
6	SS	91219	29561
7	SS	91596	29721
8	SS	91556	29098
9	SS	91606	28754
10	SS	91501	28031
11	SS	91365	27895
12	SS	91273	27959

27
WITHYPOOL, TARR STEPS & PORCHESTER'S POST

Wp	Zo	East	North
1	SS	84479	35414
2	SS	85036	35608
3	SS	85131	35052
4	SS	85743	33922
5	SS	86178	32619
6	SS	86803	32142
7	SS	85801	32021
8	SS	85282	32583
9	SS	84603	32465
10	SS	84088	32450
11	SS	83364	32968
12	SS	82859	33459
13	SS	83222	34149
14	SS	83833	34320
15	SS	84016	34459
16	SS	83451	34406
17	SS	84479	35414

28
HADDON HILL, HADDEO VALLEY & WIMBLEBALL LAKE

Wp	Zo	East	North
1	SS	96954	28519
2	SS	95873	28291
4	SS	95420	28146
5	SS	94509	27302
6	SS	95911	29263
7	SS	96178	29493
8	SS	96442	29647
9	SS	96490	30773
10	SS	96441	29247
11	SS	96808	29160
12	SS	97172	29110
13	SS	97167	28871
14	SS	96930	28496

29
COUNTY GATE & EAST LYN VALLEY TO LYNMOUTH

Wp	Zo	East	North
1	SS	79300	48654
2	SS	78645	48511
3	SS	77093	48403
4	SS	76877	48307
5	SS	74411	48806
6	SS	74208	48660
7	SS	73999	48531
8	SS	72899	48918
9	SS	72679	49026

30
CHERITON, HOAROAK WATER, EXE HEAD & PINKERY POND

Wp	Zo	East	North
1	SS	73982	47721
2	SS	73594	47499
3	SS	73239	47030
4	SS	73710	46591
5	SS	74322	45168
6	SS	74514	43501
7	SS	74757	43025
8	SS	75140	41511
9	SS	73190	41821
10	SS	72325	42211
11	SS	71654	42510
12	SS	71508	43489
13	SS	71402	44979
14	SS	72568	45161
15	SS	71929	46108
16	SS	72540	46174
17	SS	72708	47325
18	SS	73980	47724
A1	SS	74686	43060
A2	SS	73482	44362
A3	SS	73216	44996
A4	SS	72934	45693
A5	SS	72926	45973

31
EXFORD, LARKBARROW & TROUT HILL

Wp	Zo	East	North
1	SS	85480	38356
2	SS	84839	38694
3	SS	84005	39627
4	SS	82718	40292
5	SS	82401	41534
6	SS	82217	41602
7	SS	80799	40941
8	SS	79998	40857
9	SS	79077	40695
10	SS	78624	41408
11	SS	78047	41509
12	SS	79682	43315
13	SS	80369	42840
14	SS	80821	43006
15	SS	82048	42858
16	SS	83514	42223
17	SS	84607	41373
18	SS	85432	40501
19	SS	85444	38360

32
MOLLAND - ANSTEY GATE CIRCULAR

Wp	Zo	East	North
1	SS	80774	28372
2	SS	80937	28516
3	SS	81191	28829
4	SS	81391	28999
5	SS	81633	29215
6	SS	82144	29696
7	SS	82746	29906
8	SS	83502	29807
9	SS	83054	29301
10	SS	83083	28822
11	SS	82939	28690
12	SS	82841	28636
13	SS	81925	28266
14	SS	81749	28340

Wp	Zo	East	North
15	SS	81347	28303
16	SS	80796	28374

33

SIMONSBATH, EXE HEAD & CORNHAM FORD

Wp	Zo	East	North
1	SS	77398	39458
2	SS	77199	39113
3	SS	76530	39206
4	SS	76462	39266
5	SS	76485	39462
6	SS	76468	39862
7	SS	76341	40842
8	SS	75140	41512
9	SS	74875	41410
10	SS	74381	40927
11	SS	74306	39866
12	SS	73130	39983
13	SS	73375	39451
14	SS	74088	39154
15	SS	74868	38597
16	SS	75980	38642
17	SS	76084	38522
18	SS	77404	39409

34

SIMONSBATH, COW CASTLE & THE BARLE VALLEY

Wp	Zo	East	North
1	SS	77392	39441
2	SS	78158	38232
3	SS	79331	37451
4	SS	79630	37025
5	SS	80632	36394
6	SS	80648	37180
7	SS	80060	37138
8	SS	79434	38132
9	SS	78424	38802
10	SS	77388	39443

35

LANDACRE BRIDGE - WITHYPOOL CIRCULAR

Wp	Zo	East	North
1	SS	81536	36083
2	SS	82191	35835
3	SS	83068	35059
4	SS	84020	35239
5	SS	83305	35737
A1	SS	80643	36140

36

PINKERY POND & MOLE'S CHAMBER

Wp	Zo	East	North
1	SS	72858	40132
2	SS	73006	40713
3	SS	73191	41819
4	SS	72325	42212
5	SS	71649	42510
6	SS	71788	40844
7	SS	71622	40490
8	SS	71746	40032
9	SS	71779	39377
10	SS	73057	39979
11	SS	72901	40125

37

BRENDON COMMON, BADGWORTHY WATER & FARLEY WATER

Wp	Zo	East	North
1	SS	76508	43272
2	SS	77899	43549
3	SS	79568	43755
4	SS	79288	44489
5	SS	79250	45384
6	SS	78580	45622
7	SS	78260	45578
8	SS	77079	45621
9	SS	77146	45819
10	SS	75898	45039
11	SS	74814	45135
12	SS	75081	44616
13	SS	75376	44213
14	SS	75482	43723
15	SS	76393	43482

38

PORLOCK TO MINEHEAD via THE RUGGED COAST PATH

Wp	Zo	East	North
1	SS	88625	46711
2	SS	88660	46769
3	SS	88864	47310
4	SS	88933	47524
5	SS	89595	48072
6	SS	89830	48041
7	SS	89915	48948
8	SS	90551	48681
9	SS	90996	48739
10	SS	91849	48961
11	SS	93748	48416
12	SS	93976	47959
13	SS	94110	47971
14	SS	94474	47733
15	SS	94769	47689
16	SS	97026	47001
17	SS	97168	46791

39

DUNSTER, WITHYCOMBE & BAT'S CASTLE

Wp	Zo	East	North
1	SS	99278	43900
2	SS	98963	43112
3	SS	99871	42693
4	ST	00099	42220
5	ST	00308	41890
6	ST	00791	41714
7	ST	01271	41777
8	ST	01464	41339
9	ST	00555	41256
10	ST	00126	41295
11	SS	99384	41799
12	SS	98576	42495
13	SS	98983	43101

40

HORNER, HURLSTONE & PORLOCK VALE

Wp	Zo	East	North
1	SS	89775	45577
2	SS	89919	46178
3	SS	90000	46671
4	SS	90071	47620
5	SS	90180	47811
6	SS	90343	47938
7	SS	89978	48935
8	SS	89934	49012
9	SS	89244	48443
10	SS	89122	48308
11	SS	89354	47986
12	SS	88861	47304
13	SS	88665	46762
14	SS	89397	46103
15	SS	89748	45541

GLOSSARY

barrow (1) hill or hillock
(2) ancient earth-built grave mound (see *tumuli*)

clapper bridge huge slabs of stone resting on piers across rivers and streams, usually built on packhorse routes

cleave a steep-sided valley

combe a steep-sided valley often wooded and closed at one end

Devon bank field boundary constructed of a substantial earth bank topped with a hedge

hangman sandstone sedimentary rock formed from a mixture of sandstones, shales and slates, laid down in Devonian period

hanging valley wave power erodes the coastline, leaving the upper part of a valley emerging from a cliff face

herepath Saxon military road

hog's-back cliff cliff angles down before a vertical drop into the sea

layered bank /hedge saplings on bank cut and split to into layers forming new growth

leat man made channel carrying water to power water wheel

longshore drift movement of pebbles caused by currents and prevailing winds

lynchet Medieval cultivation strip caused by ploughing on a slope

motte and bailey type of castle commonly built by the Normans, on a mound (*motte*) surrounded by an (outer wall) *bailey*

saddle low point of a connecting ridge between two hills

saddleback roof steeply pitched church tower roof

sessile oak woods native British oak with stalkless acorns; was often coppiced for timber and charcoal

tumuli burial mounds (see barrow)

western (hanging) oak ancient oak woods growing on steep cliff faces; now woods often threatened by rhododendrons

whortleberry also known as bilberry or blueberry - small mauve berry growing on Exmoor, picked in July and August; known locally as 'hurts' or 'urts'

APPENDICES

Telephone numbers are shown in red, fax numbers in blue.

APPENDIX A
National Park and Tourist Information
With tourism a key part of the Exmoor economy, the region is geared up to fully support visiting walkers.
If arriving by car:
Somerset Visitor Centre   01934 750833
somersetvisitorcentre@somerset.gov.uk
Sedgemoor Services on M5 southbound

Comprehensive information is available from a network of Exmoor National Park Authority Visitors Centres, Local Information Points and Tourist Information Offices; the free 'Exmoor Visitor' magazine is an excellent fund of information.

Exmoor National Park Administrative Offices
Exmoor House
Dulverton   01398 323665 01398 323150
Somerset TA22 9HL   www.exmoor-nationalpark.gov.uk

Exmoor National Park Authority - Visitor Centres
Combe Martin
Seacot Cross St T/F   01271 883319 (seasonal opening)
      combemartinvc@exmoor-nationalpark.gov.uk
County Gate   01598 741321 (seasonal opening)
A39 Countisbury   countygatevc@exmoor-nationalpark.gov.uk
Dulverton Fore St   01398 323841
      dulvertonvc@exmoor-nationalpark.gov.uk
Dunster Dunster Steep   01643 821835 (seasonal opening)
      dunstervc@exmoor-nationalpark.gov.uk
Lynmouth The Esplanade   01598 752509 (seasonal opening)
West Exmoor
Blackmoor Gate   01598 752509

Local Information Points

Allerford Post Office	**Barbrook** Post Office
Brompton Regis Post Office & Stores	**Challacombe** Post Office
Molland Village Stores & Post Office	**Parracombe** Stores & Post Office
Simonsbath Boevey's Restaurant	**Wheddon Cross** Post Office & Stores
Winsford Stores & Post Office	**Withypool** Post Office & Stores
Wootton Courtenay The Villagers' Stores	

Tourist Information Centres

Barnstaple The Square	0845 4582003
Braunton Caen Car Park, Caen St	01271 816400
Combe Martin Seacot, 13 Cross St	01271 883319
Ilfracombe The Landmark	01271 863001
Lynton Town Hall, Lynton	01598 752225
Minehead 17 Friday St	01643 702624
Porlock Information Centre	01643 863150
South Molton 1 East St	01769 574122
Tiverton Phoenix Lane	01884 255827
Watchet 6 The Esplanade	01984 654565 (seasonal)
Woolacombe The Esplanade	01271 870554 (seasonal)

APPENDIX B
Travel
By air; the region is served by **Bristol** and **Exeter** airports.
By train; **Barnstaple** at the end of the Tarka Line connects with intercity trains at **Exeter**; the nearest main line stations are at **Taunton** and **Tiverton** Parkway.
By coach and bus; National Express routes connect to main resorts.
www.nationalexpress.co.uk
By car; the M5 runs through Somerset and Devon; for **Minehead**, exit at **Bridgwater**, Junction 24 on the A39. For the **Brendon Hills**, exit at **Taunton**, Junction 25 and follow the B3227 to **Wiveliscombe**. For **Dulverton**, southern and western Exmoor, exit at **Tiverton**, Junction 27 on A361 towards **Barnstaple**.

Local buses
Regular routes run along the A39 between **Barnstaple** and **Minehead** and the A398 between **Minehead** and **Tiverton**.
Devon Bus Nºs 309 & 310 connect **Barnstaple, Blackmoor Gate, Lynton & Lynmouth**
Quantock Motor Services Nº300 bus connects **Ilfracombe, Blackmoor Gate, Parracombe, Lynton, Lynmouth, Porlock** and **Minehead** (limited winter service).
First Bus Nº38 connects **Porlock Weir, Porlock, Minehead, Dunster** and **Watchet**.
First Bus Nº398 connects **Minehead, Dunster, Timberscombe, Wheddon**

Cross, **Dulverton** and **Tiverton**.

Limited services link villages with towns, and summer routes run to beauty spots. Three bus timetables cover the area; Taunton and West Somerset, North Devon, and Mid Devon; available from Information centres and other local outlets. South West Bus and Rail travel enquiry line 0870 608 2608
www.travelline.org.uk

APPENDIX C
Accommodation
Exmoor boasts a wide choice of accommodation, advertised widely in the national press, travel and walking magazines. Tourist Information Centres hold lists and provide a booking service for all types of accommodation including camping and caravan sites. There are plenty of self-catering holiday cottages and farms offering B&B. We live close to Exmoor so have only used overnight accommodation on a few occasions, enjoying warm welcomes and excellent facilities at **North Walk House** and **Twitchen Farm**.

North Walk House   01598 753372   northwalkhouse@btinternet.com
North Walk, Lynton EX35 6HJ

Twitchen Farm   01598 763568   www.twitchen.co.uk
Challacombe, Barnstaple EX31 4TT

Other accommodation: www.visit-exmoor.info

www.celebratingsomerset.com/visitors
'Discover Devon'   0870 608 5531

Youth Hostel Association   0870 770 8868 www.YHA.org.uk
National Customer Services (Hostels at Exford, Lynton and Minehead)

APPENDIX D
Useful Information
    www.visit-exmoor.info www.discoverdevon.com
    www.celebratingsomerset.com/visitors
Access Land   www.countrysideaccess.gov.uk

Exmoor Perambulation www.activeexmoor.com

National Trust Information
Holnicote Estate   01643 862452   holnicote@nationaltrust.org.uk
Selworthy

South West Coast Path Association
    017452 896237   www.swcp.org.uk
Lynton and Lynmouth Cliff Railway
    01598 753908
(Lynmouth from February 16 to mid November)

APPENDIX E
Bibliography
Exmoor Geology R A Edwards
    (Exmoor Books ISBN 0-86183-411-9)
Lorna Doone R D Blackmore
    (Wordsworth Classics ISBN 1-85326-076-2)

South West Coast Path Guide

(South West Coast Path Association ISBN 0-907055-08-7

updated annually)

Portrait of Exmoor J H B Peel
(out of print)
South West Coast Path Minehead to Padstow
(Aurum Press ISBN 1-85410-415-2)
The Field Archaeology of Exmoor Hazel Riley and Robert Wilson-North
(Exmoor Books ISBN 1-873592-58-2)
The Heritage of Exmoor R A Burton
(ISBN 0951441906)
The Old Mineral Line R J Sellick
(Exmoor Press ISBN 0-900131-39-X)

APPENDIX F
Long Distance Trails passing through Exmoor

Coleridge Way (36 miles) **Nether Stowey** to **Porlock**
www.exmoor –nationalpark.gov.uk/index

Macmillan Way West (102 miles) **Castle Cary** to **Barnstaple**
www.macmillanway.org

South West Coast Path (630 miles) **Minehead** to **Poole**
www.swcp.org.uk

Tarka Trail (180 mile figure of eight) from **Barnstaple**

Two Moors Way (102 miles) **Lynmouth** to **Ivybridge**

Samaritan's Way (130 miles) **Bristol** to **Croyde Bay**

Further information about these routes is available on:
www.somerset.gov.uk/celebratingsomerset/routefinder/

APPENDIX G
Attractions/Things to do

Narrow Gauge Railway, Woody Bay Station
01598 763487   www.lynton-rail.co.uk
The Lyn Valley Art & Craft Centre
Old Methodist Church, next to Town Hall
Lynton   01598 752549

Exmoor Safari
The Exmoor White Horse Inn
Exford   01643 831229

Wimbleball Lake Watersports Centre
Near Dulverton   01837 871565   www.swlakestrust.org.uk

Lynton and Lynmouth Cliff Railway
01598 753908   www.cliffrailwaylynton.co.uk

West Somerset Railway steam train
01643 704996   www.west-somerset-railway.co.uk

Allerford Rural Life Museum
01643 862529
Glen Lyn Gorge hydro electricity

Lynmouth   01598 723207

Horse riding   www.equinetourism.co.uk

Exmoor Falconry & Animal Farm
Allerford   01643 862816

Farmers' Markets (9.30-12 Noon)
With a farming tradition, Exmoor has a plethora of fresh local produce
Combe Martin Third Saturday of the month, Village Hall, High St
Minehead First & third Fridays of the month URC Church Hall, Banck St
Lynton First Saturday of the month, Town Hall, Lee Road
Minehead Country Market every Friday 9.30-11.30 Friends Meeting Hse, Banck St.

APPENDIX H
Inns and Tea Rooms
In the interest of exhaustive research, if not for the benefit of our waistlines, we've sampled and recommend:

Bossington	Kitnor's Tea Room	01643 862643
Brendon	Rockford Inn	01598 741214
Countisbury	Exmoor Sandpiper Inn	01598 741358
Dulverton	Lewis's Tea Room	01398 323850
Dunster	Luttrell Hotel	01643 821555
Heddons Valley	Hunters Inn	01598 763230
Horner	Horner Tea Gardens	01643 862380
Luxborough	Royal Oak Inn	01984 640319
Lynton	Cliff Top Café	01598 753366
Molland	London Inn	01769 550269
Monksilver	Notley Arms	01984 656217
Parracombe	Fox & Goose	01598 763621
Porlock	Ship Inn	01643 862507
Porlock Weir	Anchor Hotel & Ship Inn	01643 862753
Ralegh's Cross	Ralegh's Cross Inn	01984 640343
Selworthy	Periwinkle Cottage Tea Room	01643 862506
Simonsbath	Exmoor Inn	01643 831341
Simonsbath	Boevey's Tea Room	01643 831622
Tarr Steps	Tarr Farm Inn	01643 851507
Watersmeet	National Trust Tea Room	01271 850887
Wheddon Cross	Rest & Be Thankful Inn	01643 841222
Winsford	Bridge Tea Rooms	01643 851362
Winsford	Royal Oak	01643 831506
Withypool	Tea Rooms	01643 831178

Walk! Wire-O Spiral Bound Guidebooks are designed to be used with:

- DWG's plastic slipcover (PSC), which prevents the binding from catching on pockets and increases durability -
- - and our clear plastic All Weather Book Bag (AWBB) with grip-top seal which allows the book to be folded back displaying 2 pages, then sealed, impervious to weather conditions.

To obtain your PSC and AWBB for this book, send a C5 (9 x 7 inch) SAE with 47p stamp, to:

(Code 9781904946186)
Discovery Walking Guides
10 Tennyson Close
Northampton NN5 7HJ